WASHINGTON, DC

CONDENSED

 tom given

LONELY PLANET PUBLICATIONS
Melbourne • Oakland • London • Paris

contents

Washington, DC Condensed
1st edition – May 2002

Published by
Lonely Planet Publications Pty Ltd
ABN 36 005 607 983
90 Maribyrnong St, Footscray, Vic 3011, Australia
www.lonelyplanet.com or AOL keyword: lp

Lonely Planet offices
Australia Locked Bag 1, Footscray, Vic 3011
☎ 613 8379 8000 fax 613 8379 8111
e talk2us@lonelyplanet.com.au
USA   150 Linden St, Oakland, CA 94607
☎ 510 893 8555 Toll Free: 800 275 8555
fax 510 893 8572
e info@lonelyplanet.com
UK   10a Spring Place, London NW5 3BH
☎ 020 7428 4800 fax 020 7428 4828
e go@lonelyplanet.co.uk
France   1 rue du Dahomey, 75011 Paris
☎ 01 55 25 33 00 fax 01 55 25 33 01
e bip@lonelyplanet.fr
www.lonelyplanet.fr

Design Emily Douglas Editing Vivek Waglé, Valerie
Sinzdak and Emily K Wolman Maps Gina Gillich,
Bart Wright, Annette Olson and Stephanie Sims
Cover James Hardy and Emily Douglas Publishing
Manager Diana Saad Thanks to Gabrielle Green,
Nadine Fogale, Charles Rawlings-Way, Annie Horner,
Susan Rimerman, Tom Downs, Hayden Foell

Photographs
Many of the images in this guide are available for
licensing from Lonely Planet Images:
e www.lonelyplanetimages.com

Front cover photographs
Top: The White House
(Peter Ptschelinzew)
Bottom: The American Flag
(Eric L Wheater)

ISBN 1 74059 353 7

Text & maps © Lonely Planet Publications Pty Ltd 2002
Grateful acknowledgment is made for reproduction
permission: © Washington Metropolitan Transit Authority
Photos © photographers as indicated 2002
Printed by The Bookmaker International Ltd
Printed in China

how to use this book

SYMBOLS

- ✉ address
- ☎ telephone number
- Ⓜ nearest Metro station
- 🚆 nearest train station
- 🚌 nearest bus route
- 🚗 auto route, parking details
- ⊘ opening hours
- ⓘ tourist information
- $ cost, entry charge
- e email/website address
- ♿ wheelchair access
- 🧒 child-friendly
- ✗ on-site or nearby eatery
- V good vegetarian selection

COLOR-CODING

Each chapter has a different color code that is reflected on the maps for quick reference (eg, all Highlights are bright yellow on the maps).

MAPS

The fold-out maps inside the front and back covers are numbered from 1 to 6. All sights and venues in the text have map references which indicate where to find them on the maps; eg (5, B4) means Map 5, grid reference B4. Although each item is not pinpointed on the maps, the street address is always indicated.

PRICES

Price gradings (eg $10/5) usually indicate adult/discount entry charges to a venue. Discount prices can include senior, student, member or coupon discounts.

THE AUTHOR

Tom Given

Tom Given first saw Washington from the back-back seat of his family's station wagon. He's been back to DC again and again to visit friends, to conduct business and to attend demonstrations. In order to research *Washington, DC Condensed* he finally went back as a sightseer, covering almost every block from the Marine Corps Barracks to the far sides of Rock Creek Park to bring you the enduring pleasure of the US capital.

Thanks to David Bass, John Christie, Joe & Mary Ann McCain, Roberta McCain, Jerry Newberry and the offices of Senator Dianne Feinstein and Senator John McCain. Thanks, too, to Tom Downs, Gabrielle Green, Annette Olson and Bill Wilkinson.

READER FEEDBACK

Things change – prices go up, schedules change, good places go bad and bad places improve or go bankrupt. So, if you find things better or worse, recently opened or long since closed, please tell us and help make the next edition even more accurate. Send all correspondence to the Lonely Planet office closest to you (listed on p. 2) or visit e www.lonelyplanet.com/feedback.

facts about washington, dc

There is a white marble tower called the Washington Monument, but the entire city of Washington is a monument to the 'American Experiment.' From the cathedral of democracy on Capitol Hill in the center of town to the National Cathedral on the Northwest hills, the institutions here reflect the glory of the country and house the nation's treasures. Marble buildings line broad avenues, recalling the splendor of Imperial Rome. Smartly dressed men and women bustle about, late for meetings at the World Bank or press conferences at the National Education Association.

Beyond the great buildings, quiet streets lined with brick houses recall the coziness of small-town Southern life. Neighbors sit on porches and stoops, smoking and talking, seemingly unconnected to the institutions around the corner.

But not everybody has been seduced by the slow pace of life here, especially those trying to get something done. Forty years ago, John Fitzgerald Kennedy ribbed the city for its combination of 'Northern charm and Southern efficiency.' This tension between the two Washingtons – the world capital and the county seat – still holds today. The person next to you on the bus may bury her eyes in briefing notes for a meeting at the Defense Intelligence Agency, but when she gets off the bus she takes the time to thank the driver.

Washington wouldn't be Washington without the monuments, but Washington wouldn't be Washington either without the dogwoods and cherry trees and redbrick sidewalks. See the town inside the city, and understand how Washington seduces visitors from every walk of life.

The Tidal Basin complements the classical curves of the Jefferson Memorial.

HISTORY

Small groups of Algonquin Indians were living in the Washington area when the English settled nearby at Jamestown in 1607. Seven years later, settlers sent the first shipments of tobacco back to England, and five years after that they imported the first African slaves to work the fields. By 1627, planters were exporting a half-million pounds of tobacco a year. In 1634, the Crown granted Lord Baltimore a charter for a Catholic colony in Maryland, on the north side of the Potomac River, and in 1637 the first British Catholic colonists planted stakes in the New World.

By the mid-18th century, plantations lined the rivers of Virginia and Maryland. Prosperous river ports sprouted on either side of the Potomac River at Alexandria and Georgetown. As tensions with Britain mounted, Virginia planters like George Washington, Thomas Jefferson, James Madison and George Mason joined Boston merchants and farmers to lead a revolution. With help from the French, Washington's army defeated the British at nearby Yorktown, and a new nation was born.

Sunset lights up a colonial-style house.

A City in the Wilderness

The new nation's new capital was the product of a political compromise. Northerners wanted the capital to be Philadelphia or New York, but they also wanted Southerners to help pay their debts from the Revolutionary War. Southern states, which had paid their own war debts, were willing to assume Northern debts in exchange for a Southern capital city. Thomas Jefferson and Alexander Hamilton forged a deal to put the capital in a new federal territory somewhere on the Potomac. George Washington chose the exact site upstream from his home at Mount Vernon, Virginia.

French architect Pierre L'Enfant laid out a grand city in the wilderness. The new capital, with a Capitol Building and a President's Mansion, opened for business under John Adams, the nation's second president, in 1800. British soldiers burned the settlement during the War of 1812, and it grew back slowly until the Civil War.

The Town Grows Up

In 1861, the election of Abraham Lincoln as president and the secession of Virginia from the United States put Washington on the front lines of the Civil War. Even while Union (Northern) and Confederate (Southern) forces fought across Northern Virginia and Maryland, Lincoln never abandoned his capital. When the war ended in April 1865, the town was finally a city, standing at the center of a reunited nation.

The industrial boom of the late 1800s brought new settlers, including the middle class and the wealthy, who built townhouses and mansions around Dupont Circle. Construction of the Cairo Apartments just ten blocks from the White House triggered the 1901 McMillan Plan, which included height limits on new buildings (10 stories downtown, eight stories elsewhere) and mandated construction of new federal buildings in the fashionable beaux arts style along the National Mall and the Pennsylvania Ave corridor between the Capitol and the White House.

The Modern City

The McMillan plan came just in time. The city exploded during WWI, during the Depression, and again during WWII. The population grew from under 300,000 in 1900 to over 800,000 in 1950. After the war, 'white flight' to the new suburbs began, with white residents beating a path away from the city center, especially after the desegregation of public schools in the mid-1950s. By 1960, Washington was the first major American city with a predominantly black population.

Middle-class African Americans joined the move to the suburbs after the riots that followed the assassination of Martin Luther King Jr in April 1968. Those left behind – an increasingly poor inner-city population – suffered through one of the most difficult periods in the city's history: by the 1980s, Washington had become the 'murder capital' of the country; a corrupt mayor, Marion Barry, went to jail after video cameras caught him smoking crack with a prostitute; and Congress took financial control of the city.

In the 1990s, the city's fortunes improved, as immigrants from overseas and newcomers from elsewhere in America settled in the District. The crime rate dropped, property values rose and gentrification pushed the boundaries of 'safe' neighborhoods. The terrorist attack on the Pentagon on September 11, 2001, closed some attractions and scared away visitors, but hotels began to fill again by the end of 2001 and the city seemed poised to recover. While crime remains a problem and District finances still need help, Washington's city is once more a place to live, not just to visit.

Trundling along on the Tourmobile provides a good survey of DC's 'greatest hits.'

ORIENTATION

The District of Columbia straddles the fall line on the Potomac, where the coastal plain meets the Appalachian foothills. L'Enfant centered the city of Washington on Capitol Hill, a small rise between the Potomac and the Anacostia River.

The city is divided into Northwest, Northeast, Southwest and Southeast quadrants by N Capitol, S Capitol and E Capitol Sts and the National Mall, radiating from the Capitol on the four compass points. Numbered streets run north and south. Lettered streets – A through W, no B or J – run east and west. Avenues named after states run diagonally every which way across this grid. Addresses run 100 to the block, so 700 G St NW is at the corner of 7th St NW, 14 blocks from 700 G St NE.

The Mall runs west from the Capitol, past the Washington Monument to the Potomac. It's the country's front lawn, lined with museums and filled with memorials. Most of what there is to see lies here and in the neighborhoods to the north, from Downtown and Dupont Circle west to Georgetown.

ENVIRONMENT

Good planning by L'Enfant, and good follow-up by McMillan and Lady Bird Johnson (among others), have left Washington with a multitude of parks, most maintained by the National Park Service and the US taxpayer.

There's no heavy industry – that's up north in Baltimore – and there's lots of rain to wash the skies clean of auto exhaust. Government work hours are staggered to even out car traffic, and government subsidies have built a good subway system that offers alternatives to driving. Traffic in the suburbs, where most of the people in the metropolis live and work, is a serious problem that gets critical when accidents or emergencies close a freeway or a bridge.

Height limits inside the District assure plenty of light and air, but they do sap vitality from city streets by limiting densities in the most vibrant parts of town. It's a small price to pay when one considers the alternatives just across the Potomac: soulless clumps of towers in Crystal City and Rosslyn, notable mostly for their views of Washington.

Great Falls provides a majestic setting for paddlers and hikers.

GOVERNMENT & POLITICS

In the 1870s, Georgetown, Washington City and Washington County merged into the single unit of the District of Columbia, ruled by a board of commissioners appointed by Congress. A hundred years later, the District achieved a measure of self-government, electing its own mayor and city council. The first years of home rule, under the notorious Mayor Marion Barry, were a mixed blessing: public payrolls swelled, but the quality of public services declined.

In response to Barry's corrupt administration, Congress took away much of his power to govern the city, but legislators have returned control to new Mayor Anthony Williams, a can-do leader who was elected by a coalition of whites and blacks in 1998. Despite Mayor Williams' far-reaching popularity, the divide between white Washington west of Rock Creek Park and black Washington elsewhere remains a factor in political (and social) life.

Did You Know?
- More people work in DC (620,000) than live in DC (570,000).
- Over 20 million people visited in 1999.
- More than 60,000 lobbyists populate the Washington area.
- More than 39,000 lawyers work in the District.
- A one-bedroom apartment in a safe neighborhood costs $900-1400 per month.
- Almost 30% of DC is set aside as federal parkland.
- The crime rate for the metropolitan area is 15% lower than the national average.

ECONOMY

Washington is first and foremost a company town. About 30% of the workforce in the District, some 185,000 people, works for the federal government. The business and financial worlds employee tens of thousands, and the technology industry has lately surpassed the

Rick Gerharter

Running from Watergate is still popular.

federal government as the largest employer in the metro area. Almost 50,000 people work in the hospitality sector, driven by the city's visitor and convention businesses.

Washington is also an educated town. More than 17% of the adult population inside the District has earned graduate degrees – a higher percentage than any state in the US – and nearly three-quarters of the 2.5 million workers in the metro area hold white-collar jobs.

Home to the headquarters of Black Entertainment Television, DC is also a base for black business in America; more African American executives, administrators and managers work here than just about any other US city.

SOCIETY & CULTURE

Even before the political compromise that placed the new nation's capital on the banks of the Potomac, area residents have straddled some of the deepest divides in American culture.

The Potomac marks the first divide, between Maryland Catholics and Virginia Anglicans. This split survives today. The Maryland suburbs, home to institutions like the National Institute of Health, lean liberal while the Virginia suburbs, home of the Pentagon and CIA, tend to be conservative.

The Mason-Dixon line between Maryland and Pennsylvania, north of DC, marks the original divide between North and South. Washington may look and feel like a small Southern city once you leave the federal monuments behind, but it's also a border town.

The deepest divide, as elsewhere in America, is between blacks and whites. African Americans have been here since the first English settlers imported the first slaves. From the end of the Civil War to the end of WWII, about a quarter of the city's population was black. As whites began to move out of the city in the 1950s, African Americans grew from a minority group to a majority. This shift exacerbated a predominantly white Congress' tendency to neglect city affairs in favor of national matters; it also accelerated the flight of business from downtown to the suburbs and left the city sharply split between the prosperous, largely white Northwest quadrant (beyond the moat of Rock Creek Park) and the rest of the town.

Finally, there's a divide between those who have lived here a long time and those who come to work for the government. Many locals ignore newcomers until they stay for some period of time, and newcomers in turn sometimes spurn the locals as provincials.

Rock Creek Park provides pastoral tranquility in the heart of the city.

Etiquette

The city's Southern heritage shows up frequently (though inconsistently); you're likely to hear 'yes, ma'am' and 'no, sir' as often as 'please' and 'thank you.'

Don't expect Southern charm from drivers behind the wheel. They are probably even more lost than you are and in a hurry to get through the traffic circle. Jaywalk very carefully if you must.

Tobacco was the first cash crop here, and smokers still light up just about anywhere outside of stores and offices.

ARTS

Forty years ago, no one took the Washington arts scene seriously. It was, after all, the place where the Daughters of the American Revolution refused to let Marian Anderson sing at Constitution Hall on the eve of WWII, just because she was black.

Then the Kennedys came to town. President Kennedy read and wrote books. Mrs Kennedy invited serious artists to perform at the White House and employed other serious artists to restore the White House to its Federal-era glory. Following their example, Lyndon Johnson pushed through funding for the national center for the arts that became the Kennedy Center.

Today, 'art' is no longer a sus-pect word. You'll find great nation-al institutions as well as small neighborhood groups competing for your attention from one end of Greater Washington to the other.

The Kennedy Center's Grand Foyer

Architecture

Central Washington may be the best single work of the beaux arts design-ers of the turn of the last century. Individual buildings range from the gra-cious (John Russell Pope's West Wing of the National Gallery) to the banal (the Federal Triangle along Pennsylvania Ave between 7th and 14th Sts NW), but the overall effect is sensational.

The Federal row houses of Georgetown and Alexandria and the Victorian mansions and row houses of Dupont Circle and Kalorama offer a sampler of 19th-century vernacular architecture. The 20th-century structures in the city are frequently dreadful (the FBI Building), occasionally inspiring (the National Cathedral) and usually boring (any office building on K St NW). If you're looking for great modern architecture, this is not your town.

Literature

Washington is filled with writers, but most of them are busy running down rumors of who is doing what to whom over which piece of legislation. Not surprisingly, the memoir is the most common book about Washington (see 'Washington Stories,' p. 62), followed by political exposés such as the note-worthy *All the President's Men*, written by Carl Bernstein and Bob Woodward.

Amid the high-stakes drama of international politics, some area writers have specialized in page-turning escapist fare. Tom Clancy, of nearby Northern Virginia, produces best-selling thrillers sometimes set among the political classes. To learn more about the contemporary literary scene here, check out David Cutler's *Literary Washington: A Complete Guide to the Literary Life in the Nation's Capital*.

Theater

Until recently, the Washington theater scene was best known for Mr Lincoln's last night on the town (he was assassinated in Ford's Theatre). Shows on the way to Broadway occasionally stopped here on tryouts, and national touring companies of big Broadway shows passed through on their way to Dallas and Duluth, but that was about it. National shows still visit the refurbished National Theater, Warner Theater, and (yes) Ford's Theatre, but there are also homegrown shows aplenty these days at nonprofit institutions like the Arena Stage, Shakespeare Theatre, and Kennedy Center.

Film

With its role as the center of political intrigue secure, Washington has taken its star power to the silver screen ever since films went on location. Classics set in DC include *Born Yesterday*, the 1950s comedy that stars Judy Holliday and William Holden and takes a black-and-white look at the capital before ethics committees and air conditioning. Dustin Hoffman and Robert Redford portray crusading reporters in *All The President's Men*, the thriller about Woodward and Bernstein breaking the Watergate story. Michael Douglas plays the president and Annette Bening his lobbyist love interest in *The American President*, a romantic comedy set in the White House.

Music

One of the wellsprings of jazz in the early 20th century, Washington can claim the late, great Duke Ellington as a native son. He grew up in the Shaw district, home to the 1200-seat Howard Theater, which provided a showcase for African American talent 20 years before the Apollo opened in Harlem, New York City. Audiences migrated to the larger Lincoln Theater in the 1920s, until DC theaters were desegregated after WWII.

Jazz aside, the DC music scene never attracted much attention until 1971, when the Kennedy Center threw open the doors to its enormous concert halls. Today, classical music and opera thrive there and at Virginia's Wolf Trap Farm Park for the Performing Arts. Meanwhile, jazz and blues joints still hum from U St to Georgetown, and rock is resurgent in clubs along the U St/14th St corridor and amid the warehouses of the Southeast quadrant.

The Duke and other jazz greats gave DC a reputation as the 'Harlem of the South.'

highlights

Sightseeing in DC is mainly a matter of museums and monuments. From the Capitol to the National Gallery to the Smithsonian to the National Zoo, America's heritage is on display. Most everything is free – the US taxpayers cover the bills – but the busier attractions give out tickets for crowd control. Security questions – a big issue before September 11, 2001, and an even bigger issue afterward – can lead to sudden closings of streets and buildings. Government funding – a mystery anytime – can temporarily close this attraction or that. The key word for the whole process is 'patience.' Buy the pass of your choice for the Metro to avoid testing your patience by driving, get comfortable walking shoes for the hikes between attractions, carry something to read if you get stuck in a line and you'll be all right.

While you're at it, save time to explore the city behind the great monuments. You'll find grand houses, magnificent parks and sidewalk cafes and restaurants that allow you to watch the world as you rest and refuel. See what people are wearing and listen to what people are saying – you'll get insight into the mixture of Richmond and Rome that draws visitors to DC, whatever the political or economic clime of the time.

Stopping Over?

One Day Start at the Capitol (if it's open) or Library of Congress (if it's not). Walk over to Union Station for lunch, then take the Red Line to Dupont Circle to visit the Phillips Collection. Window-shop around the neighborhood before dining and clubbing or coffeehouse-ing in Adams-Morgan.

Two Days Spend the morning at the Smithsonian and lunch at the food court in the Ronald Reagan Building/International Trade Center. Head to Arlington National Cemetery in the afternoon, then return to the city for dinner and postdinner clubbing around Dupont Circle.

Lowlights of Washington

Our (admittedly subjective) least favorite aspects of visiting Washington include the following:

- summer heat and humidity
- constant worries about personal security
- lines at major attractions
- food trucks serving the same dreary fare from one end of the Mall to the other
- absence of a real downtown shopping district
- traffic circles: you can't get under 'em (on foot) and you can't get over 'em, so you'll just have to go around and around.
- shortage of taxis after dark and of parking spaces anytime

Rick Gerharter

Uninspired architecture, another lowlight

Three Days Spend the morning at the National Gallery and have lunch at the Sculpture Garden Pavilion Café. Walk down the Mall past the Vietnam Veterans Memorial and Lincoln Memorial to the Kennedy Center and Georgetown. Dine in Georgetown, then take in a jazz or classical performance.

ARLINGTON NATIONAL CEMETERY (4, G4)

Arlington National Cemetery is an evolving monument to modern American history, from the golden days of Old Virginia to the dark hours of the 1960s. It's also – more importantly – an evolving monument to the men and women who died in American wars from the Revolutionary War to the present day. Here, on 200 of the most beautiful acres in the world lie over 260,000 graves and memorials, ranging from humble headstones for runaway slave soldiers to the **everlasting flame** for JFK.

INFORMATION

✉ Memorial Dr off George Washington Pkwy, Arlington, VA
☎ 703-607-8052
ℯ www.arlington cemetery.org
Ⓜ Arlington Cemetery
⊘ Oct-Mar 8am-5pm, Apr-Sept 8am-7pm
⑨ free
ⓘ 40min Tourmobile tour $5.25/2.50; fresh-cut flowers permitted on graves anytime; no photography permitted at or near funerals
⅏ yes
✕ food court at Pentagon City Mall (1100 S Hayes St; ☎ 703-415-2400)

Lee Foster

The final resting place of America's fallen

Arlington's rendezvous with American history began in 1778, when George Washington's stepson, John Parke Custis, acquired the site upstream from Mount Vernon. His son built **Arlington House** between 1802 and 1818, and his granddaughter, Mary Anna, married Lt Robert E Lee here in 1831. When the Civil War broke out, the Lees left the estate and Union forces moved in. The estate was confiscated in 1864, and the quartermaster of the Union Army began burying Union dead on the front lawn.

The Lees never returned, and burials of Civil War veterans continued throughout the 19th century. Arlington became a national cemetery during the Spanish-American War. It began housing the **Tomb of the Unknown Soldier** after WWI.

Burial Rights

Not every veteran can be buried in Arlington. With space at a premium, burial or internment is limited to members of the armed forces who die on active duty or retire from active duty, members of the armed forces who earn a medal while on active duty, and prisoners of war. Spouses, widows and widowers are also eligible, as are presidents, former presidents and justices of the US Supreme Court.

John Fitzgerald Kennedy was buried on the hill below Arlington House in November 1963. In 1968, Robert F Kennedy was buried nearby, under the only wooden cross in the cemetery. Jacqueline Kennedy Onassis was buried next to her husband after her death in 1994.

GEORGETOWN   (4, C4)

Before there was a District of Columbia, there was Georgetown. English settlers built a tobacco port here in the 1700s on the site of an Indian village. When the federal government set up shop in the area in 1789, local gentry moved in, along with Jesuit priests who founded Georgetown University on the hill west of town.

Before and during the Civil War, Georgetown was a Confederate hotbed. It was also home of a free black community. The **Mount Zion United Methodist Church** is the oldest African American church in the District. The entrance to its small cemetery is tucked alongside the apartments at 2513 Q St, just west of Rock Creek.

Georgetown merged with the rest of the District of Columbia in 1871 and went into decline until the 1930s, when government workers employed by Franklin D Roosevelt's New Deal began buying and rehabbing local row houses. The Kennedy family moved into Marbury House, on N St NW, in the 1950s, and Georgetown came back into style. Residents such as the late *Washington Post* matriarch Katharine Graham

INFORMATION

- ✉ bounded by Rock Creek on the east, Georgetown University on the west, R St on the north & Potomac River on the south
- ☎ 944-5295
- e www.georgetowndc.org
- Ⓜ Foggy Bottom/GWU (10-15min walk); Georgetown shuttle every 10mins from Foggy Bottom/GWU, Dupont Circle & Rosslyn Metro stations (fare 50¢, or 25¢ with Metro transfer)
- ♿ yes
- ✗ Dean & DeLuca (p. 64)

(who lived on R St) and her sidekick Ben Bradlee have kept the Georgetown area fashionable – particularly among the liberal intelligentsia – ever since.

You'll find the best shopping in the District here, from clothes and jewelry to art and antiques. You'll also have your choice of a wide range of restaurants, from sandwich shops for college students to bistros for ladies who lunch.

Most of all, you'll find charming old houses on quiet tree-lined side streets. Just watch your step – the brick sidewalks are treacherous – and enjoy.

Fall is starkly elegant in Georgetown.

DON'T MISS
- C&O Canal (p. 41) • Dumbarton Oaks (p. 37)
- Potomac shore at Washington Harbour • Tudor Place

JEFFERSON MEMORIAL (5, K5)

The man who modestly asked to remembered only as 'Author of the Declaration of American Independence, of the Statute of Virginia for Religious Freedom, and Father of the University of Virginia' would be pleased by the beauty of this building but horrified by the fact that such a grand structure was a memorial to his life.

INFORMATION

- ✉ 900 Ohio Dr SW
- ☎ 426-6841
- e www.nps.gov/thje
- Ⓜ Smithsonian
- ⏰ 24hrs
- $ free
- ⓘ park ranger programs offered 8am-11:45pm
- ♿ yes
- ✗ Captain White's Seafood City (1100 Maine Ave SW;
  ☎ 484-2722)

Based on the Parthenon in Rome and Jefferson's library at the university, the Jefferson Memorial was dedicated by President Franklin Roosevelt in 1943, on the 200th anniversary of Jefferson's birth. A 19ft likeness by Rudulph Evans stands in the center of the large, airy rotunda. The inscription inside the dome immortalizes one of Jefferson's most famous vows: 'I have sworn upon the altar of God eternal hostility against every form of tyranny over the mind of man.' Side panels on the rotunda walls bear portions of the Declaration of Independence.

The small exhibit space in the basement below highlights portions of the life of this country's ultimate Renaissance man. (JFK once told a gathering of US Nobel Prize winners that they were the greatest assembly of talent to meet in the White House since Thomas Jefferson dined alone.)

The front steps of the memorial offer one of the best views in a city filled with views – across the water of the Tidal Basin to the Washington Monument, the Ellipse and the White House beyond. It's powerful anytime but particularly in spring, when the cherry trees bloom, or on warm summer nights.

Both Jefferson and his Memorial have been known to engage in tranquil reflection.

KENNEDY CENTER   (4, E2)

The John F Kennedy Center for the Performing Arts is a living memorial to a man who was arguably the most sophisticated American president of the 20th century. Initially authorized as a National Cultural Center during the Eisenhower administration, it was named for JFK after his assassination in November 1963. It opened for business in September 1971 with the performance of Leonard Bernstein's 'Mass,' commissioned for the occasion.

The center's seven performance spaces play host to major cultural luminaries that include the National Symphony Orchestra, the Washington Opera Company and the American Film Institute. Its 1100 full-time employees present over 3200 performances every year in spaces as large as the 2450-seat **Concert Hall** and as small as the 250-seat AFI screening room. Although there are other performance spaces in the city, all of them combined can't match the breadth or depth of the offerings here.

Kennedy Center Awards

Every year since 1978, the Kennedy Center has honored men and women for their lifetime contributions to American culture. The first recipients – Marian Anderson, Fred Astaire, George Balanchine, Richard Rogers and Arthur Rubenstein – set the standard for those who followed. Recipients for 2001 were Julie Andrews, Van Cliburn, Quincy Jones, Jack Nicholson and Luciano Pavarotti.

A 'living memorial': DC's Kennedy Center

INFORMATION

- ✉ 2700 F St NW
- ☎ 416-8340
- e www.kennedy-center.org
- Ⓜ Foggy Bottom/GWU; free shuttle from Metro Mon-Sat 9:45am-midnight, Sun & holidays noon-8pm
- ⊘ tours Mon-Fri 10am-5pm, Sat-Sun 10am-1pm; box office open Mon-Sat 10am-9pm, Sun & holidays noon-9pm
- Ⓢ free
- ⓓ yes
- ✕ Kennedy Center Café, Roof Terrace Restaurant

Tucked behind the on-ramps to I-66, the building can be hard to find. Once you do get there, you can enjoy the promenade along the Potomac bank and the views from the river and roof terraces. Stroll the grand hallways, the Hall of Nations and the Hall of the States. The **Grand Foyer**, along the river side, is longer than the Washington Monument is tall.

If you're short on money or time, take in the free performance at the Millennium Stage in the Grand Foyer at 6pm nightly.

LIBRARY OF CONGRESS (5, G14)

The Library of Congress is more than just the largest collection of books and documents in the world. Its 1897 Jefferson Building is also an extravagant beaux arts creation that would be worth a visit even if it were empty.

The library was founded in 1800, when John Adams persuaded Congress to spend $5000 to buy 'such books as may be necessary for Congress' in the brand-new city that had neither bookstores nor libraries. Two years later, Thomas Jefferson persuaded Congress to create the post of Librarian of Congress, appointed by the President, and to establish a budget for the library to acquire books on a regular basis.

When British troops invaded Washington in 1814, they burned the library with the rest of the city. To replace the loss, Jefferson offered Congress his personal library at cost, and the legislators had the good sense to accept. For $23,490, the Library received over 6000 volumes, assembled by the most active mind of his time.

In 1870, the Library's future was assured when Congress required every applicant for a copyright to deposit with the Library two copies of anything presented for copyright. Today, the collection includes over 120 million items, including 18 million books, 12 million photos, 2.5 million recordings, and 54 million documents. The stacks are closed, but the entire collection is available for anyone to view in one of the 20 reading rooms. No references or recommendations are required, just a photo ID.

INFORMATION

- ✉ 101 Independence Ave SE
- ☎ 707-8000
- ⓔ www.loc.gov
- Ⓜ Capitol South
- ⏰ Jefferson Building exhibits Mon-Sat 10am-5:30pm, Madison Building exhibits Mon-Sat 8:30am-9:30pm
- Ⓢ free
- ⓘ tours of Jefferson Building Mon-Sat 10:30 & 11:30am, 1:30, 2:30 & 3:30pm (no 3:30pm Sat); reader's cards available for anyone over 17 in the Madison Building, Room L140
- ♿ yes
- ✕ Madison Building cafeteria

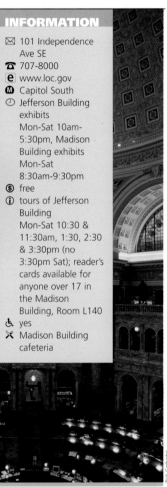

Your school librarian's wildest fantasy...

Rick Gerharter

DON'T MISS
- Jefferson's original book collection • three-story Main Reading Room
- World Treasures exhibit • Gutenberg Bible

LINCOLN MEMORIAL (5, G2)

The Lincoln Memorial closes the west end of the picture-postcard view down the Mall from the US Capitol and the Washington Monument. The great neo-Greek temple features 36 columns for the 36 states of the Union at the time of Lincoln's death. Inside is a statue of a seated Abraham Lincoln by Daniel Chester French – a familiar sight to many Americans, but strangely stirring in the huge, quiet space of the memorial chamber.

This temple to the man who saved the nation that he called 'the last best hope on Earth' is as plain and elegant as his words. Inscribed along the south wall of the chamber is his famous Gettysburg Address, a 272-word masterpiece of oratory commemorating more than 7000 soldiers who lost their lives in the battle that helped save the Union and free the slaves. Along the north wall of the chamber run the words of Lincoln's second inaugural address, directing us to act 'with malice toward none, with charity for all.'

Below the memorial chamber, a small display space houses an exhibit on Lincoln's Washington and on the memorial itself. A small bookstore on the memorial chamber level offers both the standard assortment of postcards and books about the Great Emancipator.

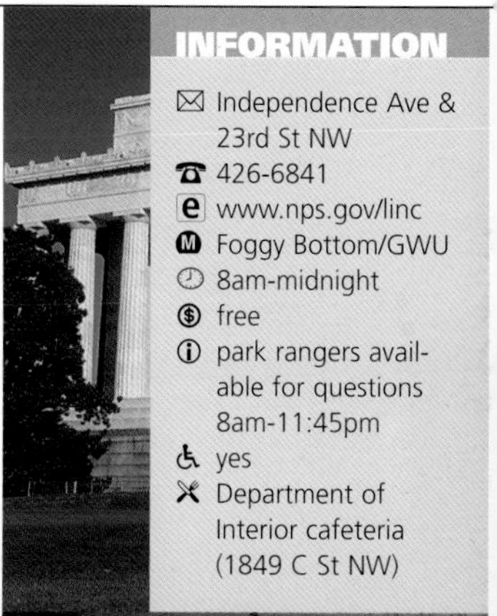

Rick Gerharter

INFORMATION

- ✉ Independence Ave & 23rd St NW
- ☎ 426-6841
- e www.nps.gov/linc
- M Foggy Bottom/GWU
- ⌚ 8am-midnight
- $ free
- ⓘ park rangers available for questions 8am-11:45pm
- ♿ yes
- ✗ Department of Interior cafeteria (1849 C St NW)

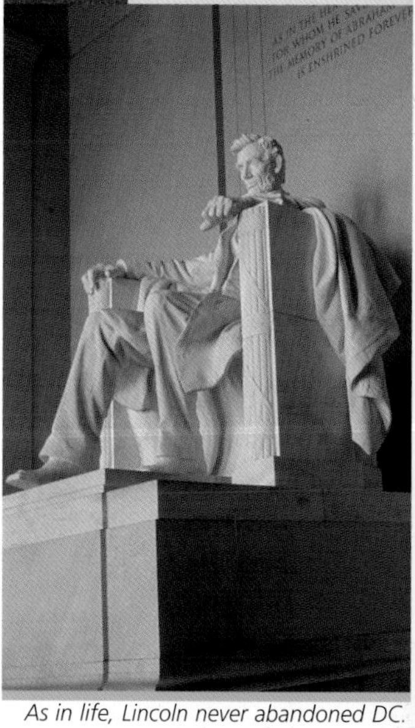

Rick Gerharter

As in life, Lincoln never abandoned DC.

Symbol of Freedom

The Lincoln Memorial has served as a symbol of civil rights ever since the black president of Tuskegee Institute was seated separately from white speakers at the opening ceremonies in 1922, spurring protests by outraged African Americans. The famous black contralto Marian Anderson sang here when the Daughters of the American Revolution barred her from Constitution Hall in 1939. Martin Luther King Jr delivered his historic 'I Have a Dream' speech at the memorial during the March on Washington in 1963.

NATIONAL AIR & SPACE MUSEUM (5, H10)

This immense glass box on the National Mall is a love letter to mankind's dreams of flight. From historic aircraft like the Wright Brother's biplane and Lindbergh's *Spirit of St Louis* to historic spacecraft like the Apollo 11 command module *Columbia*, one hundred years of flight are laid out before you.

Rick Gerharter

INFORMATION

- ✉ 7th St & Independence Ave SW
- ☎ 357-1400
- e www.nasm.edu
- Ⓜ L'Enfant Plaza, Smithsonian
- ⏱ 10am-5:30pm
- Ⓢ admission free (entry tickets required at peak times); IMAX films $6.50/5.50 (IMAX tickets can be purchased 2 weeks in advance); Einstein Planetarium $4; combination passes available
- ⓘ audio tours in five languages $5/4.50
- ♿ yes
- ✗ Pavilion Café at the National Gallery (p. 21)

Scores of aircraft hanging in midair dazzle the eye, while exhibits on everything from African Americans in aviation to WWWII combat dazzle the mind. Replicas of Robert Goddard's first rocket, the first Russian Sputnik satellite and the first US Explorer satellite display how far the exploration of space has come in such a short time.

The **Langley Theater** shows five different IMAX films throughout the day, from the groundbreaking, early IMAX picture *To Fly* to newer films like *The Magic of Flight* and *Adventures in Wild California*. The acrophobic may want to wait outside, or line up instead for one of the **Einstein Planetarium** shows, such as *And a Star to Steer Her By*, a history of navigation narrated by Alec Guinness.

Gluttons for airplanes can also visit the museum's **Paul E Garber Facility**, a few miles southeast of the District in Suitland, Maryland. You'll find over 150 aircraft stored in five hangars. In 2003, this collection will be moving to a new facility at Dulles airport, which will house over 300 aircraft, including the *Enola Gay*, which dropped the atomic bomb on Hiroshima. Advance reservations are required for the Garber tours; call two weeks ahead.

Success! The Wright brothers' plane

Rick Gerharter

DON'T MISS
- Breitling Orbiter 2 Gondola (circumnavigated Earth) • *Bell XI* (broke sound barrier) • simulated flight deck of US Navy carrier

NATIONAL GALLERY OF ART   (5, G10)

The National Gallery is one of the brightest stars in the Washington cultural firmament. Founded in the 1930s by financier Andrew Mellon, it opened for business in 1941 and quickly attracted gifts from other American connoisseurs, such as Samuel Kress, to form one of the best collections in the country.

After outgrowing the original neoclassical **West Building**, the National Gallery expanded into the **East Building** in 1978. That's where you'll find modern art (from the early 20th century to the present day); older art (from the Middle Ages through late impressionism) resides in the West Building.

This is one of the few places in North America where one can see large numbers of European paintings from the 16th, 17th and 18th centuries, produced in Germany and the Low Countries, as well as France, England and Italy. There are great paintings here, by Rembrandt and Titian and Vermeer, and solid works by lesser-known artists that would be the stars of lesser collections. This is home, too, to one of the best selections of early American paintings, from Gilbert Stuart's familiar portraits of Washington and Jefferson to Rembrandt Peale's portrait of his brother Rubens.

The modern work on display ranges from the Matisse cutouts in the tower to paintings by Pollock, Johns and Rauschenberg to wonderful Calder mobiles. Both buildings also house temporary exhibits on anything from Goya's images of women to prints from Gemini GEL in Los Angeles (the country's best print studio).

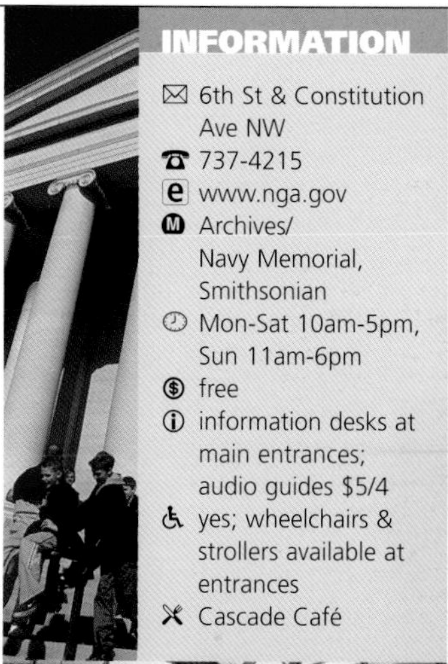

INFORMATION

- ✉ 6th St & Constitution Ave NW
- ☎ 737-4215
- e www.nga.gov
- Ⓜ Archives/ Navy Memorial, Smithsonian
- ⊘ Mon-Sat 10am-5pm, Sun 11am-6pm
- Ⓢ free
- ⓘ information desks at main entrances; audio guides $5/4
- ♿ yes; wheelchairs & strollers available at entrances
- ✗ Cascade Café

Rick Gerharter

Rick Gerharter

A Calder mobile greets passersby.

DON'T MISS
- Cézanne's *Bend in the Road* • Raphael's *Small Cowper Madonna*
- Picasso's *Family of Saltimbanques*

NATIONAL ZOO (4, A5)

The National Zoo rambles over 163 acres in Rock Creek Park, with outdoor habitats and indoor exhibits strung along 5 miles (8km) of paved trails.

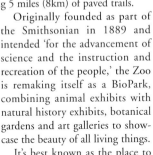

INFORMATION

- ✉ 3001 Connecticut Ave NW
- ☎ 673-7800
- e www.si.edu/natzoo
- Ⓜ Woodley Park/Zoo
- 🕐 zoo grounds May 1-Sept 15 6am-8pm, Sept 16-April 30 6am-6pm; zoo buildings May 1-Sept 15 10am-6pm, Sept 16-April 30 10am-4:30pm
- $ free
- ⓘ visitor information centers off Connecticut Ave & Rock Creek Pkwy entrances; guided tours Sat-Sun morning by reservation (☎ 673-4956)
- ♿ yes; strollers & wheelchairs available
- ✗ Mane Restaurant

Rick Gerharter

Originally founded as part of the Smithsonian in 1889 and intended 'for the advancement of science and the instruction and recreation of the people,' the Zoo is remaking itself as a BioPark, combining animal exhibits with natural history exhibits, botanical gardens and art galleries to showcase the beauty of all living things.

It's best known as the place to see giant pandas from China. The first pandas arrived in 1972, after Nixon went to China. The current residents, Mei Xiang and Tian Tian, arrived in December 2000, after Ling-Ling and Hsing-Hsing died here at ages 23 and 28, respectively. The Zoo has joined a worldwide effort to breed pandas in captivity before their natural habitats disappear completely.

Pachyderm podiatry is a prickly pastime.

Lions and tigers and bears live here, too, plus apes, bats and birds and a whole host of animals who come from far and wide – the American prairies, Australia and Amazonia. Entrance to some exhibits can be limited when the zoo is particularly crowded. Get there early in the morning, before the animals take their midday siestas, and wear sunscreen and comfortable shoes.

DON'T MISS
- Komodo dragons • Golden Lion tamarins • Reptile Discovery Center • beaver pond

ROCK CREEK PARK (6, E5)

Rock Creek Park provides a slice of country in the middle of the city – 1800 acres of forest and glens running from the Potomac River to the Maryland border, where it joins 2700 more acres in Rock Creek Regional Park. Set aside by Congress in 1890, this large park divides the Upper Northwest from the rest of Washington.

Rock Creek is a perfect city park, with picnic sites, a golf course, a tennis center and educational facilities such as the **Nature Center**. An array of hiking trails stretches for 29 miles (46km), bridle paths meander for 12 miles (19km) and bike trails run for 10 miles (16km) – and that doesn't even include **Beach Drive**, which is closed to cars on weekends.

It's a history park, as well, with two Civil War forts, the cabin of poet Joaquin Miller and a couple of burial grounds in the narrow neck of the Rock Creek valley south of the National Zoo.

Most of all, though, Rock Creek is a wilderness park. The hills along the east side and the rocky ledges inside mark the boundary between the Atlantic coastal plain and the Piedmont hill country, which leads up to the Blue Ridge Mountains west of town. Get away from the parkway that runs through the bottom of the valley and you'll find yourself in dense second-growth forest. Oaks and poplars, hickories and dogwoods reach skyward, as alders, witch hazel and azaleas fill out the understory.

As Washingtonians underuse the park, visitors can take advantage of its relative solitude and tranquility.

INFORMATION

- ✉ Upper Northwest btw 16th St & Connecticut Ave NW, from Potomac River btw Georgetown & Kennedy Center northwest to Maryland border
- ☎ 282-1063
- e www.nps.gov/rocr
- Ⓜ Woodley Park/Zoo, Cleveland Park, Friendship Heights
- ◴ park sunrise-sunset, Nature Center Wed-Sat 9am-5pm
- ⑤ free
- ⓘ visitor information at Police Station (Beach Dr south of Military Rd) & Nature Center (5200 Glover Park Rd NW, south of Military Rd)
- ✗ Woodley Grill

Pierce Mill dates back to 1794.

 DON'T MISS
- Carter Barron Amphitheater • Perrier parcourse (exercise circuit)
- planetarium • Pierce Mill

SMITHSONIAN INSTITUTION   (5, H8)

The word 'Smithsonian' means different things to different people – to some, a redbrick warehouse filled with mementos like Charles Lindbergh's airplane; to others, a natural history museum stuffed with gems and dinosaur bones. Still others think of 'Smithsonian' as a set of art museums showing work by everyone from the 19th-century Japanese artist Hokusai to pop painter Roy Lichtenstein.

The Smithsonian is all of these things, and much more. Encompassing 14 museums and galleries in Washington, two other museums in New York City, and the National Zoo in Rock Creek Park, it's the world's largest collection of museums, plus a research and educational facility that publishes books and magazines, develops television and radio programs and produces exhibits and lectures that travel around the world.

Inside Washington, 'Smithsonian' usually refers to the nine museums and galleries strung along the National Mall – the Arts & Industries Building, the Hirshhorn Museum and Sculpture Garden, the Freer Gallery, the

National Air and Space Museum (p. 20), the National Museum of African Art, the National Museum of American History, the National Museum of Natural History, the Sackler Gallery and the Smithsonian Institution Building. But the Smithsonian also includes the National Postal Museum (p. 45), the National Zoo (p. 22) and the Renwick Gallery (p. 35), all located elsewhere in the city.

With so much to see, it's hard to know where to start. Many visitors begin at the 1855 Smithsonian Institution Building, better known as **the Castle**, the original home

INFORMATION

- ✉ 1000 Jefferson Dr SW
- ☎ 357-2700
- e www.si.edu
- Ⓜ Smithsonian
- ◷ 10am-5:30pm (extended summer hrs)
- $ free
- ⓘ main information center in the Castle, other centers in separate museums
- ♿ yes
- ✕ food court in Ronald Reagan Building (1300 Pennsylvania Ave NW)

Dennis Johnson

Smithson's Will

The Smithsonian Institution is the creation of a man who never set foot in America. In 1829, English chemist James Smithson left his fortune to his nephew with the proviso that, if the nephew died without an heir, the fortune would go to the government of the USA to found 'at Washington, under the name of the Smithsonian Institution, an establishment for the increase and diffusion of knowledge among men.' Six years later, the nephew died childless, but it took Congress a decade longer to set aside its anti-British prejudices (which had thrived after the War of 1812) and accept Smithson's gift. In 1855, the redbrick castle designed by James Renwick opened for business on the south side of the National Mall.

Gareth McCormack

Adventures in Wonderland? No, it's the equally magical Smithsonian Castle.

of the Institution. Two theaters show a 24-minute orientation video, and interactive terminals present programs on the Institution in six languages.

Even more visitors start at the **National Museum of Natural History**, which has passed the National Air and Space Museum as the biggest visitor attraction in town. Some come to gawk at the famous Hope Diamond, the largest blue diamond in the world, while others head straight to the Dinosaur Hall to visit triceratops and T-rex. Children drag parents to the insect zoo to pet tarantulas.

Just to the west, the **National Museum of American History** documents American life, real and fictional, with artifacts from Dorothy's ruby slippers in *The Wizard of Oz* to Muhammad Ali's boxing gloves. Exhibits explore historical events like the post–Civil War Great Migration of African Americans, and a collection of objects commemorates presidents. You'll see the desk on which Jefferson drafted the Declaration of Independence and the hat Lincoln wore the night he went to Ford's Theatre.

Across the Mall, four great art museums delight the eye and the mind. The **Freer Gallery** may be the most interesting. Its collection of Asian and late-19th-century art shows how much American painters like Whistler owed to the Chinese and Japanese. The South Asian and East Asian art in the **Sackler Gallery** and the collection in the **National Museum of African Art**, next door, offer a lively counterpoint to the European and American work in the nearby National Gallery.

The aggressively modern profile of the **Hirshhorn Museum** advertises its collection. You'll see both now-classic work from Diebenkorn, Stella and O'Keeffe and still-modern art by Kiefer, Kapoor and Nauman. The pieces in the adjoining **Sculpture Garden** range from small works by Degas and Daumier, kept indoors, to Rodin's *Burgers of Calais.* All promise to warm the soul. If modern art always leaves you cold, you haven't been here.

DON'T MISS
• Freer's Peacock Room • Galapagos IMAX film in Natural History Museum • Benin bronzes in Museum of African Art

US CAPITOL   (5, G13)

This is the grand temple of democracy, looming over the city from the hill between the Potomac and the Anacostia, just as L'Enfant and Washington envisioned. It's the place where the people's representatives meet to do the people's business, and it's the place where the people themselves can stop in and watch their representatives at work.

Like the country it embodies, the Capitol has grown by fits and starts over the years. An amateur architect, Dr William Thornton, designed the original building in classical style. In 1793, George Washington laid the cornerstone. The north wing was almost completed when Congress arrived from Philadelphia in 1800. The south wing, for the House of Representatives, debuted in 1807. A wooden walkway connected the two, awaiting a central domed building, when British troops burned the structure in 1814. Reconstructed Capitol wings opened in 1819, followed in 1826 by the center, topped with a low wood-and-copper dome by Charles Bullfinch, architect of Boston's State House.

By 1850, both the Senate and House had outgrown their chambers as the number of states in the Union passed 30. Congress was persuaded to add two grand wings to each end of the original set of buildings and to top the center building with a cast-iron dome 287ft (86m) tall. The House moved into its new

INFORMATION

- ✉ 1st & Capitol Sts NE
- ☎ 225-6827
- e www.cr.nps.gov, www.aoc.gov
- Ⓜ Capitol South, Union Station
- ⊘ Mar-Aug 9:30am-8pm, Sept-Feb 9am-4:30pm
- ⑤ free
- ⓘ guided tours every half hour 9:30am-3:30pm (line up on the south side of E Capitol St); self-guided tours admitted in small groups every 5min (line up on the north side of E Capitol St)
- ♿ yes
- ✕ Senate & House cafeterias, Union Station food court (50 Massachusetts Ave NE)

Rick Gerharter

chamber in 1857, the Senate into its in 1859, just in time for the Civil War. Lincoln insisted that work continue on the dome throughout the war, as a symbol of Union determination. On December 2, 1863, the 19ft (6m) Statue of Freedom rose up to crown the dome's top.

At the close of the 19th century, the first House and Senate office

Visitors' Galleries

The House and Senate galleries are usually open when the bodies are meeting, even if the rest of the building is on partial lockdown for security reasons. US citizens can get passes from their representatives or senators. Write in advance or drop by their offices. Overseas visitors can obtain passes from the House appointment desk or the Senate appointment desk, both on the 1st floor of the building.

buildings were built on either side
of the Capitol grounds, linked to
the Capitol by tunnels and electric
subways. Finally, between 1958
and 1962, the entire East Front of
the building grew by 32ft (10m).
Today, the Capitol includes over
500 rooms. Some 20,000 people
work in and around it, including
535 legislators and more than
1200 Capitol police.

> ### Capitol Gardens
> The Capitol sits in acres of gardens
> designed by Frederick Law Olmsted,
> who laid out a series of terraces on
> the west face of the building to create
> a grand view down the Mall. The
> reflecting pool at the bottom of the
> terraces is actually a roof over I-395
> below. The beautification efforts con-
> tinue to this day, with the ongoing
> construction of a new National Gar-
> den next to the Botanic Garden, at the
> corner of Independence Ave & 1st St
> SW. It will include a rose garden, a
> water garden and an environmental
> garden, in keeping with these times.

The Capitol's interior decoration matches the grandeur of its
outside. Constantino Brumidi's
fresco *The Apotheosis of George
Washington* adorns the Rotunda, as
does a Brumidi frieze that was
completed in 1953, years after his death. The **Rotunda** also features eight
large historical paintings by John Trumbull, and statues from all 50 states
grace **Statuary Hall**. Fussy 19th-century wood- and metalwork lend elegance to the walls, doorways and ceilings throughout the buildings.

All this remains remarkably accessible, even after September 11, 2001.
The Capitol is unique in achieving that democratic goal for 200 years, just
by opening its doors and letting the people stroll in.

The Capitol in its adolescence: Charles Bullfinch's original, relatively modest dome

US HOLOCAUST MEMORIAL MUSEUM (5, H6)

The Holocaust Memorial Museum is one of the two most moving attractions in Washington. Whereas the Vietnam Veterans Memorial presents only a blank slate in the middle of the grass, leaving everything to the visitor's imagination, the Holocaust Museum takes the visitor by the hand, actively helping him or her to imagine the unimaginable. Neither memorial ever fails to stir its audience.

INFORMATION

- ✉ 14th St & Independence Ave SW
- ☎ 488-0400
- e www.ushmm.org
- Ⓜ Smithsonian
- ⓞ 10am-5pm; closed Yom Kippur
- Ⓢ free (but timed-entry tickets required for permanent exhibit, available daily at museum or in advance through e www.tickets.com or ☎ 800-400-9373)
- ♿ yes
- ✕ museum café

At the Holocaust museum, the visitor's journey begins on the ground floor. You hand in your ticket, pick up a small passport with the story of one person who went through the Holocaust and take the elevator to the 4th floor, where the permanent exhibit begins. As you descend floor by floor, as though descending into the horrors of the time, you turn the pages of the passport to uncover another chapter of your companion's real-life journey through hell.

The top floor of the permanent exhibit chronicles the rise of the Nazis. The middle floor recounts the Final Solution, from the first ghettos and massacres to the industrialization of killing. The 1st floor recalls the final death

The Holocaust Museum's somber facade

marches, the liberation of the camps and the rebirth of the State of Israel. Chilling artifacts help to evoke the time, including a railroad boxcar used to ship Jews to the camps, piles of luggage from the warehouses of Auschwitz and a collection of photos from a single Jewish community.

Tips for Sensitive Travelers

The permanent exhibit does not pull any punches telling its story. However, the most graphic images sit behind barriers that screen the sensitive material from children and visitors who don't want to look. The exhibit for children on the ground floor is a good alternative for adults who are readily upset.

US SUPREME COURT   (5, G14)

If the US Capitol is the great temple of democracy, then the Supreme Court is the holy of holies. Almost everything about the Court speaks to the near-sacred importance of law in a secular democracy, from the majesty of its home to the capital 'C' in its name.

Your pilgrimage begins on arrival. First, walk up broad white marble steps to a magnificent portico with eight huge pairs of Corinthian columns, the architrave reading, 'Equal Justice under Law.' Then head through the enormous bronze doors (and security) into the Great Hall, lined with busts of the former chief justices. Finally, at the end of the hall, you reach the court chamber itself, two side-by-side cubes decorated in red and white that together are 44ft (13m) high, 91ft (27m) wide and 82ft (25m) deep.

If you're lucky enough to be in Washington when the Court is in session (October to June), you can line up to see the justices at work hearing oral arguments. Choose between the three-minute section (for those who just want a quick look at the process) and the longer-stay section (for those who want to hear an entire argument). If you're in Washington when the Supremes are on vacation, you can hear a lecture on the Court inside the courtroom.

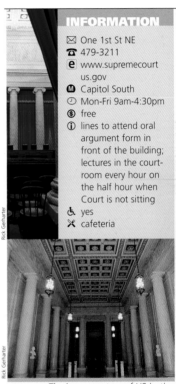

INFORMATION

✉ One 1st St NE
☎ 479-3211
ⓔ www.supremecourt
   us.gov
Ⓜ Capitol South
🕐 Mon-Fri 9am-4:30pm
⑤ free
ⓘ lines to attend oral
   argument form in
   front of the building;
   lectures in the court-
   room every hour on
   the half hour when
   Court is not sitting
♿ yes
✗ cafeteria

Rick Gerharter

Rick Gerharter

The inner sanctum of US justice

On the ground floor of the building, you'll find a good exhibit on the history of the Court, displays on high courts worldwide and a small theater showing a film on the Court.

Marshall and *Marbury*

In 1803, the Court's first chief justice, John Marshall, took on a case involving the Judiciary Act of 1789 and declared that the statute was unconstitutional – beyond the power of Congress – and therefore invalid. This decision, *Marbury v Madison*, was a milestone in world history, the effective birth of a court system independent of a king or a legislature.

VIETNAM VETERANS MEMORIAL   (5, G3)

Five years after the last helicopters left the US Embassy in Saigon, Congress set aside a corner of the lawn near the Lincoln Memorial for a memorial to the veterans who fought in Vietnam. That fall, a competition to design the memorial began; any US citizen 18 or over could try his or her hand at one of the most daunting of tasks. On May 1, 1981, a jury of eight artists and designers reviewed 1421 entries and unanimously chose the design submitted by Maya Lin, a 21-year-old Asian American college student.

The committee's choice ignited a controversy reminiscent of the war itself. Lin's design – two polished black-granite walls inscribed with the names of the dead and missing – didn't call for a conventional bronze figure of men in action. Some likened it to a black scar that insulted, rather than celebrated, the sacrifices of the soldiers. After months of debate, though, the dissenters gave up their protests when a group led by H Ross Perot offered to pay for a traditional sculpture nearby.

After 20 years, Lin's design has stood the test of time. Night and day, visitors stream to the plain black gash in the soft green lawn. Their reflections in the wall link them almost physically with the names on the wall. Some come to find the name of a friend or a relative among the 58,000 on the wall, to leave a note or a flower or make a rubbing of the inscription. Others simply come to view the honor roll of men and women who gave their last full measures in a war that did not have the full support of their country.

INFORMATION

- ✉ 21st St & Constitution Ave NW
- ☎ 426-6841
- e www.nps.gov/vive
- Ⓜ Foggy Bottom/GWU
- ○ 8am-midnight
- ⑤ free
- ⓘ directories of the names on the wall available at ranger station 8am-11:45pm
- ♿ yes
- ✕ food trucks on Constitution Ave

Rick Gerharter

Finding the Fallen
The names of the dead and missing are listed chronologically according to the dates they became casualties, starting at the middle of the monument where the two walls meet. Names marked with diamonds are confirmed as dead. Names marked with crosses are missing.

Rick Gerharter

WASHINGTON MONUMENT (5, G6)

The shaft of the Washington Monument looms over all of Washington, reflecting the sun from morning to night and blinking its little red eyes from night to morning. It's a fitting memorial to a man who would not be king and who would not serve more than two terms in the novel post of US president.

Construction began in 1848 on a spot due west from the Capitol and almost due south of the White House (the spot exactly due south was too marshy to build on). It proceeded slowly at first, due to problems raising money and hanging on to materials (Pope Pius IX contributed a block of marble that was promptly stolen by Catholic-haters). When the Civil War broke out, the monument was a mere stub a couple of hundred feet high in the middle of a field full of cattle waiting to be slaughtered to feed nearby Union troops.

The Army Corps of Engineers (later responsible for the beaux arts splendor of the Library of Congress) took over the work in 1876 and finished it eight years later. A faint line in the shaft marks the transition where the Corps switched from one kind of white marble to another.

The shaft is 555ft (167m) tall and 55ft (17m) wide at its base. Elevators speed visitors to the observation landing near the top, for the best view in Greater Washington. You can walk the 897 steps back down if you dare.

INFORMATION

- ⊠ 15th St btw Jefferson Dr & Constitution Ave NW
- ☎ 426-6841
- e www.nps.gov/wamo
- Ⓜ Smithsonian
- ☻ 1st Sun in Apr to Labor Day 8am-11:45pm, other times 9am-4:45pm
- Ⓢ free (but timed-entry tickets required; available from kiosk on 15th St side)
- ♿ yes
- ✗ food court in Ronald Reagan Building (1300 Pennsylvania Ave NW)

Rick Gerharter

Dennis Johnson

Cherry Trees

In 1912, the mayor of Tokyo gave Washington 3000 Yoshino cherry trees as a gesture of friendship. Planted along Potomac Park's reclaimed shores, they took root in the heart of the city. Every spring hundreds of thousands of locals and visitors come for cherry-blossom time, as they would back in Japan.

THE WHITE HOUSE (5, E5)

It's one thing to see the White House in photographs or postcards. It's another thing entirely to see the famed building sitting behind the fences on Pennsylvania Ave or the Ellipse. And it's a third thing altogether to walk though the public rooms of the White House and experience firsthand this curious combination of a presidential palace and a home.

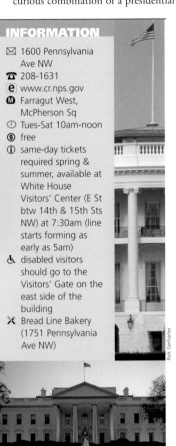

INFORMATION

- ✉ 1600 Pennsylvania Ave NW
- ☎ 208-1631
- e www.cr.nps.gov
- Ⓜ Farragut West, McPherson Sq
- ⊘ Tues-Sat 10am-noon
- Ⓢ free
- ⓘ same-day tickets required spring & summer, available at White House Visitors' Center (E St btw 14th & 15th Sts NW) at 7:30am (line starts forming as early as 5am)
- ♿ disabled visitors should go to the Visitors' Gate on the east side of the building
- ✗ Bread Line Bakery (1751 Pennsylvania Ave NW)

Rick Gerharter

Home and workplace of the top dog

Rick Gerharter

Like the Capitol, at the other end of Pennsylvania Ave NW, the White House was designed by an architect selected in a competition run by George Washington and Thomas Jefferson. The winner, James Hoban, was born and trained in Ireland. He based his design of this Georgian building on a villa in Dublin. Washington oversaw the construction, and his successor, John Adams, became the first resident when the capital moved from Philadelphia in 1800.

The original building has been repaired and expanded countless times since. Dolley Madison painted it white to cover the damage after the British burned Washington in 1814. Theodore Roosevelt added the East Wing for office space. The Trumans almost completely rebuilt the structure, and Jacqueline Kennedy restored the public rooms with historic art and furniture.

The end result boasts the scale of a gracious country house and the look of a small museum. The tour is self-guided, so you can linger as long as you like, but the currents of people coursing through the rooms can drag you along, so it's best to peruse the free pamphlet and know what you want to see before you clear security, to get the most out of your visit.

DON'T MISS
- Gilbert Stuart's portrait of George Washington • Duncan Phyfe furniture in Green Room • view of North Portico from Northeast Gate

sights & activities

Visitors' Washington is a small slice of a small town, 1 or 2 miles (2 or 3km) wide and 3 or 4 miles (5 or 6km) long. It's easy to cover on foot or by Metro. The terrain is basically flat; the biggest obstacles you're likely to find are traffic and traffic circles.

Capitol Hill, the center of L'Enfant's city, lies at its far east end. People working on the Hill fill the charming row houses in the heart of the area; very poor and dangerous districts surround the edges. **The Mall**, the grassy promenade running west from the Capitol, is lined with great museums and boring government office buildings.

Downtown lies north of the Mall and Pennsylvania Ave. The old part of Downtown, east of 15th St NW, has come back from a near-death experience, with new shops and clubs enlivening the area. The newer part of Downtown to the west is dull day or night, save for a good assortment of restaurants and great nightspots toward its north end near Dupont Circle.

Dupont Circle and the outer edge of the inner city, from **Woodley Park** to **Adams-Morgan** to the **New U Corridor** just beyond, are the most interesting neighborhoods in town. They're the heart of the gay community, a hub for Ethiopian immigrants and a center of old-time society.

Across Rock Creek in Upper Northwest, mainly white Washington runs from **Georgetown**, home to an upscale university, into increasingly suburban areas, ending at the Friendship Heights Metro and the Maryland state line.

Far from the Maddening Crowd

You'll find big crowds and long lines if you hit town during high season, but there are plenty of places to take a break even on the busiest days. If the weather is good, sneak off to the **Hirshhorn Museum and Sculpture Garden** (p. 25), **Lafayette Square**, across from the White House, or the Potomac shore near **Washington Harbour**. If it's too hot, cold or wet, try the West Building of the **National Gallery** (p. 21) – it's free and filled with benches – or one of the coffeehouses along 7th St NW or Dupont Circle.

Those crazy documents that began it all: the National Archives

MUSEUMS

B'nai B'rith Klutznick National Jewish Museum (5, B5)

Three exhibit rooms house changing shows on Jewish life in North America. The permanent displays include a letter from George Washington to Moses Seitas, head of the Sephardic Jewish community in Newport, Rhode Island, affirming religious liberty in the new American republic.

⊠ 1640 Rhode Island Ave NW ☎ 857-6583 ℮ www.bbinet.org Ⓜ Farragut North or Dupont Circle ⊙ Sun-Thurs 10am-5pm, Fri 10am-3:30pm; closed Jewish holidays ⑤ free ⅋ good

'I coulda painted that!'

Rick Gerharter

Corcoran Gallery

(5, E5) The largest private art museum in Washington is also the oldest art museum of any kind in DC and the only professional art and design school in the city. Best known for its collection of 19th-century American paintings, the Corcoran deserves equal attention for temporary shows that feature works

from Romanov jewels to the Harlem Renaissance.

⊠ 500 17th St NW ☎ 639-1700 ℮ www .corcoran.org Ⓜ Farragut West ⊙ Sun-Mon & Wed-Sat 10am-5pm (Thurs to 9pm) ⑤ free ⅋ good

Folger Shakespeare Library (5, G15)

Inside a neoclassical marble box hides the great hall of an Elizabethan manor, complete with Renaissance books and the world's largest collection of printed works by Shakespeare. The small theater here recalls London's Globe Theatre. Take in the exhibits or a play or watch the scholars at work in the library.

⊠ 201 E Capitol St SE ☎ 544-4600 ℮ www .folger.edu Ⓜ Capitol South, Union Station ⊙ Mon-Sat 10am-4pm ⑤ free ⅋ yes

Hillwood Museum & Gardens (6, E5)

When her husband was stationed in Russia in the 1930s, heiress Marjorie Merriweather Post took the opportunity to acquire a large array of Russian art and artifacts. She willed the collection – the best of its kind outside Russia – plus this house and its 25 acres of gardens on the edge of Rock Creek Park 'for the benefit of future generations.' Only 250 visitors can enter per day; reservations are required.

⊠ 4155 Linnean Ave NW ☎ 686-8500 ℮ www.hillwood museum.org Ⓜ Van Ness/UDC ⊙ Tues-Sat 9am-5pm; closed Feb

⑤ $10/8/5 (no children under 12) ⅋ yes

Kreeger Museum

(4, B2) You'll need reservations and a car to visit the Kreeger and its collection of modern art, housed in the home that Philip Johnson and Richard Foster designed for the Kreegers in 1967. It's worth the effort to see work by Monet, Picasso and Stella, plus some special exhibits, in a stunning domestic setting.

⊠ 2401 Foxhall Rd NW ☎ 337-3050, reservations 338-3552 ℮ www.kreeger museum.com ▣ Foxhall Rd btw Dexter & W Sts ⊙ Tues-Sat 10:30am & 1:30pm ⑤ free ⅋ good

National Building Museum (5, D11)

The immense courtyard of the Old Pension Building, with its 75ft (23m) Corinthian columns, is worth a stop on a walk from Downtown to Capitol Hill. And the changing exhibits on the ground floor – a recent show featured the work of Schindler in Los Angeles – call for a detour from almost anywhere.

⊠ 401 F St NW ☎ 272-2448 ℮ www.nbm.org Ⓜ Judiciary Square ⊙ Mon-Sat 10am-4pm (Jun-Aug to 5pm), Sun noon-4pm ⑤ free ⅋ good

National Museum of Women in the Arts

(5, D7) Ever wonder what happened to all the women when you read your art-history textbook?

So did the founders of this museum, dedicated to often-unknown work by female artists, from the Renaissance to the present day. The paintings, sculptures and other pieces grace a magnificent former Masonic Temple, which took eight years to be restored to its present glory.
✉ 1250 New York Ave NW ☎ 783-5000
🄴 www.nmwa.org
Ⓜ Metro Center
🕐 Mon-Sat 10am-5pm, Sun noon-5pm Ⓢ $5
♿ yes

Phillips Collection
(4, C6) Inch for inch, this is the best museum in the District. In 1921, Duncan Phillips opened the first modern art museum in America to show now-classic works like Renoir's *Luncheon of the Boating Party* and Picasso's *The Blue Room*. See the creations of modern masters (O'Keeffe, Lawrence and Diebenkorn) and old masters with modern sensibilities (El Greco and Chardin).
✉ 1600 21st St NW
☎ 387-2151 🄴 www .phillipscollection.org
Ⓜ Dupont Circle
🕐 Tues-Sat 10am-5pm (Thurs to 8:30pm), Sun noon-5pm Ⓢ $7.50/4
♿ good

Renwick Gallery
(5, D5) This mansion across the street from the White House was the home of William Corcoran, founder of the Corcoran Gallery, before his collection outgrew the house. Today it houses the Smithsonian's permanent collection of American arts and crafts, plus changing exhibits on the American craft scene.
✉ Pennsylvania Ave & 17th St NW ☎ 357-2700 🄴 www.si.edu
Ⓜ Farragut North, Farragut West
🕐 10am-5:30pm
Ⓢ free ♿ yes

Textile Museum
(4, C5) George Hewitt Meyers opened this museum in 1925 with a collection of 275 rugs and 60 related bits of textile. Today, it holds over 16,000 objects from almost every corner of the world, ranging from Oriental carpets to African textiles. It's one of the best places in the world to see Coptic and pre-Columbian works.
✉ 2320 S St NW
☎ 667-0441 🄴 www .textilemuseum.org
Ⓜ Dupont Circle
🕐 Mon-Sat 10am-4pm, Sun 1-5pm Ⓢ free
♿ yes

Rick Gerharter

The Renwick, dedicated to the glory of...Sam Maloof?

GALLERIES

Almost all of the galleries in the District are clumped together along 7th St NW, around Dupont Circle or in Georgetown.

Anton Gallery (4, C6)
Contemporary ceramics, paintings, sculpture and photographs reflect an East-West sensibility here. Gallery owner Gail Enns developed a taste for Asian art as a student in the 1960s and has since curated cross-cultural shows elsewhere in Washington and in Asia.
✉ **2108 R St NW** ☎ **328-0828** @ **www.antongallery .com** Ⓜ **Dupont Circle** ⊙ **Tues-Sat 11am-5pm** ⑤ **free**

How to set off an alarm

Rick Gerharter

David Adamson Gallery/Editions
(5, E9) Lithographer David Adamson and his wife, artist Laurie Hughes, are turning their gallery into a showcase for digital prints and photography, exploring new media for a new century. Shows often feature local artists and change every six weeks or so.
✉ **406 7th St NW** ☎ **628-0257** Ⓜ **Gallery Pl/Chinatown, Archives/ Navy Memorial** ⊙ **Tues-Sat 11am-5pm** ⑤ **free**

Foundry Gallery
(4, C6) Founded by four students in 1971, the oldest artists' co-op in Washington still shows work by local artists in its galleries, which are tucked in a lane off Florida Ave, behind the Phillips Collection. It's a wider range of work than you'd find in a commercial gallery, all for sale on a wide range of terms.
✉ **9 Hillyer Ct** ☎ **387-0203** @ **www.foundry -gallery.org** Ⓜ **Dupont Circle** ⊙ **Tues-Sat 11am-5pm, Sun noon-5pm** ⑤ **free**

Fraser Gallery (2, D3)
Expect contemporary art that's realistic in content (figurative paintings, drawings, prints and photos), in tone (not too aggressive for the average patron), in scale (small enough for the average home) and in price (from a few hundred to a few thousand dollars).
✉ **1054 31st St NW** ☎ **298-6450** Ⓜ **Foggy Bottom/GWU** 🚌 **30, 32, 34, 35, 36, Georgetown shuttles** ⊙ **Tues-Fri noon-3pm, Sat noon-6pm** ⑤ **free** ♿ **yes**

Govinda Gallery
(2, D1) Painting and photography for the rock 'n' roll set, the pieces here include photos of celebrities like Patti Smith, John Lee Hooker and Robert Mapplethorpe. A recent exhibit featured the work of Korda, the Cuban photographer known for his iconic portrait of Ché Guevara.
✉ **1227 34th St NW** ☎ **333-1180** @ **www .govindagallery.com**
🚌 **30, 32, 34, 35, 36, D2, Georgetown shuttles** ⊙ **Tues-Sun 11am-6pm** ⑤ **free** ♿ **yes**

Susan Conway Gallery (2, D4)
Since she opened up shop, Susan Conway has represented artist Pat Oliphant, whose political cartoons of Richard Nixon, Patrick Moynihan and others have amused US newspaper readers for years. In addition to his work, you'll find art from 20 other well-known American artists in this historic home off the main drag in Georgetown.
✉ **1214 30th St NW** ☎ **333-6343** @ **www .artnet.com/conway.html** Ⓜ **Foggy Bottom/GWU** 🚌 **30, 32, 34, 35, 36** ⊙ **Tues-Sat 11am-5pm** ⑤ **free**

Torpedo Factory Art Center (6, J5)
Three floors of art contain 83 studios housing over 160 artists, plus another five galleries showing work from 1400 nonresidents. Whatever your interest, there's something to see – painting and sculpture, stained glass and weaving, photography and prints. If current work fails to hold your interest, the Archeological Museum also displays artifacts from the neighborhood.
✉ **105 N Union St, Alexandria, VA** ☎ **703-838-4565** @ **www .torpedofactory.org** Ⓜ **King** ⊙ **10am-5pm** ⑤ **free** ♿ **yes**

NOTABLE BUILDINGS

Once you get past the monuments, Washington's short on great architecture but long on great houses and gardens.

Anderson House

(4, C6) This grand Dupont Circle mansion has hardly been touched since the Andersons built it in 1902. It's home to the Society of the Cincinnati, founded in 1783 by officers who served under Washington; today their descendants offer the public the chance to see Revolutionary War–era artifacts, plus early-20th-century decor.
☒ **2118 Massachusetts Ave NW** ☎ 785-2040
Ⓜ **Dupont Circle** 🚌 **G2**
🕐 **Tues-Sat 1-4pm**
⑤ **free** ♿ **limited**

Dumbarton Oaks

(2, A3) The house and museum are indefinitely closed due to flood damage, but the gardens alone are worth the hike up from M St. Here you'll find sweeping lawns overlooking the Rock Creek valley, rose gardens and arbors punctuated with the sight and sound of water, all a tad reminiscent of the Great Gatsby's estate.
☒ **R St btw 31st & 32nd Sts NW** ☎ 339-6401 Ⓜ **Dupont Circle**
🚌 **30, 32, 34, 36, G2**
🕐 **Mar 15-Oct 31 2-6pm, Nov 1-Mar 14 2-5pm** ⑤ **$5/3; free Nov 1-Mar 14**

The Octagon (5, E4)

Designed by William Thornton, first architect of the Capitol, The Octagon was the temporary home of President and Dolley Madison after the British burned the White House in 1814. Now home to the museum of the American Institute of Architects, whose headquarters building wraps around the house, it combines exhibits on architecture and design with exhibits on the house itself.
☒ **1799 New York Ave NW** ☎ 638-3105
Ⓜ **Farragut West**
🕐 **Tues-Sun 10am-4pm**
⑤ **$5/3** ♿ **yes**

Old Post Office Pavilion (5, F8)

Saved from demolition, this great Romanesque Revival palace now houses the DC Chamber of Commerce Visitor Information Center, a food court and federal offices. The view from the bell-tower observation deck is one of the best in town.
☒ **1200 Pennsylvania Ave NW** ☎ 606-8691
ℯ **www.nps.gov**
Ⓜ **Federal Triangle**
🕐 **Apr-Labor Day 8am-10:45pm, Labor Day-Mar 10am-5:45pm**
⑤ **free** ♿ **yes**

The Pentagon (4, H5)

Even viewed from Pentagon City or National Airport, or glimpsed from bridges or freeways, the Pentagon looks every bit what it is: the largest office building on earth. Access and tours offered before the Sept 11, 2001, attack on its south side were suspended at press time.
☒ **Arlington, VA**
☎ **703-695-1776**
ℯ **www.defenselink.mil/pubs/pentagon**
Ⓜ **Pentagon** 🕐 **call for open hrs** ⑤ **free** ♿ **yes**

Union Station (5, E14)

When the 1901 McMillan Plan consolidated the railroad stations in the capital, well-known Chicago architect Daniel Burnham arrived to design the new terminal. He produced a white marble gateway based on the Roman Baths of Diocletian. Last renovated in the 1990s, the city's front door now sports great restaurants, a multiplex, shops and DC's best food court.
☒ **50 Massachusetts Ave NE** ☎ 371-9441
Ⓜ **Union Station**
🕐 **24hrs** ⑤ **free** ♿ **yes**

Four sides weren't good enough for the Madisons.

Rick Gerharter

MONUMENTS

The centerpiece of the revitalized New U District

African American Civil War Memorial

(4, B8) This memorial to the black troops in the Civil War includes the names of 209,145 men who served with the Union Army, including 7000 white officers, such as Robert Gould Shaw, who volunteered to serve with African American units.

✉ U St & Vermont Ave NW ☎ 667-2667
ⓔ www.afroamcivilwar.org Ⓜ U St/Cardozo
🕐 24hrs Ⓢ free ♿ yes

Franklin Delano Roosevelt Memorial

(5, J4) FDR wanted only a small memorial, the size of his desk (you can see this

Sharing FDR's love of dogs

modest slab in the sidewalk outside the National Archives). But that wasn't enough for his compatriots, who created a 7.5-acre memorial along the Potomac near the Jefferson Memorial. Four open-air rooms tell the story of his four terms as president.

✉ W Basin Dr ☎ 426-6841 ⓔ www.nps.gov/fdrm Ⓜ Smithsonian
🕐 8am-midnight
Ⓢ free ♿ yes

Gandhi Memorial

(4, C6) A statue of the Mahatma (see p. 51) graces the small park across the street from the Indian Embassy on Massachusetts Ave. In good times and bad, it serves as an informal shrine to peace in the middle of Embassy Row.

✉ Massachusetts Ave at 22nd & Q Sts NW
Ⓜ Dupont Circle
🕐 24hrs Ⓢ free ♿ yes

George Washington Masonic National Monument

(6, J5) The other Washington Monument, modeled after a lighthouse in Rome, rises 333ft (100m) above George's old stomping

grounds in Alexandria. Take the elevator to the top for one of the better views of Greater Washington or opt for the full tour and learn almost everything you wanted to know about the Masons.

✉ 101 Callahan Dr, Alexandria, VA ☎ 703-683-2007 Ⓜ King St
🕐 9am-5pm Ⓢ free
♿ yes

US Marine Corps War Memorial

(4, F3) The iconic bronze replica of the iconic photo of US Marines raising the flag over the island of Iwo Jima does more than pay tribute to the men who joined that battle. It celebrates all US Marines, who have fought in almost every fight the US ever had, from the shores of Tripoli to the present day.

✉ Meade Dr & Arlington Blvd, Arlington, VA
☎ 703-289-2500
ⓔ www.nps.gov
Ⓜ Rosslyn 🕐 24hrs
Ⓢ free ♿ yes

US Navy Memorial

(5, F9) Start with trees and waterfalls and a circular plaza ringed with masts flying semaphore flags, place a sculpture of a seaman in his pea coat in the middle, toss in a visitors' center with a display of seagoing stuff off to the side, and you've got a lovely memorial to US sailors as well as a gracious spot to stop and sit in the sun.

✉ 701 Pennsylvania Ave NW ⓔ www.nps.gov Ⓜ Archives/Navy Memorial 🕐 24hrs
Ⓢ free ♿ yes

HISTORIC SITES

Cedar Hill (4, J12)

Frederick Douglass, a major African American voice of the 19th century, lived here from 1877 to 1895. Most of the furnishings in the house date from that time. Tours by National Park Service rangers highlight Douglass' role in the struggle to abolish slavery and deliver full civil rights to black Americans.

✉ 1411 W St SE
☎ 426-5961 e www.nps.gov/frdo/cedar Ⓜ Anacostia (then transfer to bus B2)
🚌 11th St Bridge to Martin Luther King Jr Ave; turn left on W St and go 4 blocks to visitors' center parking
🕐 Apr-Sept 9am-5pm, Oct-Mar 9am-4pm
⑤ free ♿ limited

Ford's Theatre (5, E8)

On April 14, 1865, John Wilkes Booth shot Abraham Lincoln here during a performance of *Our American Cousin*. The president was carried across the street to Petersen House, where he died the following morning. Look around or take the National Park Service tours of both buildings.

✉ 511 10th St NW
☎ 347-4833 e www.nps.gov/foth Ⓜ Metro Center 🕐 9am-5pm (theater sometimes closed for rehearsals or matinees) ⑤ free ♿ yes

Fort Stevens (6, D5)

This remnant of the ring of forts that defended the capital during the Civil War is the site of the only battle fought in the District, on July 11, 1864. Lincoln came to watch and got so close that he risked being shot himself.

✉ 13th & Quackenbos Sts NW ☎ 426-6828
e www.nps.gov/cdwd/stevens 🚌 52, 53, 54
🕐 sunrise-sunset
⑤ free ♿ yes

Old Stone House

(2, D4) The oldest building in DC sits in the middle of Georgetown's shopping strip. Built in 1765, it's had a number of lives before its present incarnation as a little museum of artifacts of 18th-century life.

✉ 3051 M St NW
☎ 426-6828 e www.nps.gov/olst Ⓜ Foggy Bottom/GWU 🚌 30, 32, 34, 35, 36, Georgetown shuttles 🕐 Wed-Sun noon-5pm ⑤ free ♿ yes

Woodrow Wilson House (4, C5)

The former home of the only ex-president to retire in the District of Columbia itself, this time capsule from the 1920s offers a peek into Roaring Twenties Washington society. Be sure to take a gander at Mrs Wilson's elegant dresses.

✉ 2340 S St NW
☎ 387-4062 Ⓜ Dupont Circle 🕐 Tues-Sun 10am-4pm ⑤ free ♿ yes

Civil War Battlefields

Some of the Civil War's most important battles were fought within two hours' drive of DC. **Manassas National Battlefield Park** (1, B3; ☎ 703-361-1339; sunrise-sunset), or Bull Run, is the closest, about 30 miles (48km) west of town on I-66. Site of the war's first pitched battle, in July 1861, Manassas saw another big battle a year later. The South's victories inspired Lee to invade at Antietam Creek in Maryland and set the stage for the war's bloodiest day. Over 20,000 men died or suffered injuries at what is now **Antietam National Battlefield Park** (1, B3; ☎ 301-432-5124), about 70 miles (110km) north of Washington. Take I-70 to exit 49 and Route 40; follow Route 40 to Boonsville; turn left at Route 34 to Sharpsburg; turn right at Route 65 and proceed to the visitors' center (June-Aug 8:30am-6pm, Sept-May, 8:30am-5pm).

Rick Gerharter

HOUSES OF WORSHIP

Islamic Center of Washington (4, B5)
The national mosque for American Muslims traces the community's history. Built in the 1950s as a house of worship for foreign diplomats, it also serves a large homegrown Muslim community today. Take in the sights of Islamic art – from stunning tile work to glorious calligraphy – or the sounds of Islamic worship.
✉ **2551 Massachusetts Ave NW** ☎ **332-8343** Ⓜ **Dupont Circle** ◷ **Mon-Sat 10am-5pm, Sun 10am-2pm** Ⓢ **free** ♿ **yes**

Facing east to Mecca

Franciscan Monastery of the Holy Land
(6, E6) Monks tend the beautiful gardens here, which are filled with plants from the greenhouse on the premises. You'll find replicas of key locations from Jesus' life, a path marking the stations of the cross and even a model of the Roman catacombs (accessible only on a tour)
✉ **1400 Quincy St NE** ☎ **526-6800** Ⓜ **Brookland/CUA** ◷ **9am-5pm; tours hourly Mon-Sat**

9am-4pm, Sun 1-4pm Ⓢ **free** ♿ **yes**

Mount Zion United Methodist Church
(4, D5) The oldest African American church in DC dates from 1816, when members of Georgetown's large black community broke away from Dumbarton Methodist Church. The church organized one of DC's first schools for black children and served as a stop on the Underground Railway.
✉ **1334 29th St NW** ☎ **234-0148, tour reservations 337-6711** Ⓜ **Foggy Bottom/GWU** 🚌 **30, 32, 34, 35, 36, Georgetown shuttles** ◷ **tours by reservation only; services Sun 11am** Ⓢ **free** ♿ **yes**

National Shrine of the Immaculate Conception (6, E6)
The massive basilica and 329ft (99m) campanile of the largest Catholic church in the Americas challenge the Capitol and Washington Monument as eye-catching sights. The church is a 20th-century blend of Romanesque and Byzantine. There are seven masses on Sunday and choral performances throughout the year.
✉ **400 Michigan Ave NE** ☎ **526-8300** ℮ **www.nationalshrine.com** Ⓜ **Brookland/CUA** ◷ **Apr-Oct 7am-7pm, Nov-Mar 7am-6pm** Ⓢ **free** ♿ **yes**

St John's Church
(5, D6) Designed in 1815 by Benjamin Latrobe (one of the first architects of the US Capitol), St John's has served as the church of the presidents since James Madison's day. While not the biggest church in Washington, it is one of the most charming.
✉ **16th & H Sts NW** ☎ **347-8766** Ⓜ **McPherson Sq** ◷ **Mon-Sat 9am-3pm; tours after 11am; services 1st Sun of the month** Ⓢ **free** ♿ **yes**

Washington National Cathedral (4, A3)
The sixth-largest Gothic cathedral in the world, this Episcopalian institution hosts national events like state funerals and memorial services, and each week it offers prayers devoted to a different state and religious tradition. The tower overlook is the highest point in DC.
✉ **Massachusetts & Wisconsin Aves NW** ☎ **537-6200** ℮ **www.cathedral.org** Ⓜ **Cleveland Park** 🚌 **30, 32, 34, 35, 36, N2, N3, N4, N6, N7** ◷ **Mon-Fri 10am-5pm, Sat 10am-4:30pm, Sun 8am-5pm** Ⓢ **$5/4** ♿ **yes**

The cathedral behind bars

PARKS

Chesapeake & Ohio Canal National Historic Park (2, D4)

Designed to link the Potomac with the Ohio, the C&O Canal ran 184 miles (295km) from Georgetown to Cumberland, Maryland, but fell short of its goal. Begun in 1828, it was almost immediately outmoded by the new railroads. Today, Washingtonians and visitors enjoy hiking and biking the towpath, canoeing sections of the canal and cruising in mule-drawn canal boats (p. 56).

✉ visitors' center 1057 Thomas Jefferson St NW ☎ 653-5190 ℮ www .nps.gov/choh Ⓜ Foggy Bottom/GWU 🚌 30, 32, 34, 35, 36, Georgetown shuttles ⏲ visitors' center Apr-Oct 10am-4pm, Nov-Mar Sat-Sun 10am-4pm 💲 1hr canal boat trip $8/6/5

Kenilworth Park & Aquatic Gardens

(6, F8) Acres of gardens along the Anacostia River revolve around water lilies and other aquatic plants. Come in June, when the day-blooming lilies are peaking, or July and August, when their night-blooming cousins wake up from their sleep.

✉ 1650 Anacostia Ave btw Quarles & Douglas Sts NE ☎ 426-6905 ℮ www.nps.gov/nace/ keaq Ⓜ Deanwood 🚌 New York Ave (Hwy 50) toward Annapolis; exit Kenilworth Ave (I-295 south); right on Douglas St, just after exit ⏲ 7am-4pm 💲 free ♿ yes

Meridian Hill Park

(3, C5) Also known as Malcolm X Park, Meridian Hill is the first rise above the coastal plain. Find great views and a beautiful series of fountains and cascading pools. Look for children's events and concerts during the summer and drumming Sundays in good weather.

✉ 16th St btw W & Euclid Sts NW Ⓜ Dupont Circle, U St/ Cardozo 🚌 S1, S2, S4 ⏲ sunrise-sunset 💲 free ♿ yes

National Arboretum

(6, F7) This 446-acre park on the Anacostia's west bank features all manner of trees, shrubs and flowering plants. It's best known for its Bonsai Museum. A 40min tram tour is offered weekends Apr to Oct.

✉ 3501 New York Ave NE ☎ 245-2726

℮ www.usna.usda.gov 🚌 New York Ave to Bladensburg Rd; right to R St; left to park entrance ⏲ 8am-5pm 💲 admission free, tram tour $3/2/1 ♿ yes

Theodore Roosevelt Island Park (4, E4)

The great outdoorsman would be delighted with these 91 acres of woods in the middle of the Potomac. There's a small plaza and memorial to TR, but the rest of the island is untouched, left for birdlife, waterlife and human spectators.

☎ 703-289-2500 ℮ www.nps.gov/this Ⓜ Rosslyn 🚌 I-66 over Potomac to George Washington Memorial Pkwy north; exit for parking lot just past interchange ⏲ sunrise-sunset 💲 free ♿ limited

The Capitol Columns huddle up in the Arboretum.

The National Mall

The 300ft-wide (90m) green expanse that serves as the nation's front lawn has had a past more worthy of a backyard: over the last 150 years, it's been a stockyard and a railroad yard, among other things. But what was designed as a great avenue has returned to a more fitting purpose. Today, world-class museums and marble federal buildings line the Mall, spanning the distance between the Capitol and the Washington Monument.

COLLEGES & UNIVERSITIES

Catholic University of America (6, E6)
In 1884, the Roman Catholic bishops of the USA petitioned the Pope to open a Catholic university in America. Their wish was granted in 1890. CUA educates all sorts of students but still focuses on producing teachers and professionals to lead the American Catholic community.
✉ **620 Michigan Ave NE** ☎ **319-5305** 🅴 **www.cua.edu** Ⓜ **Brookland/CUA** ⊘ **tours Mon-Fri 10:30am & 2pm from Admissions Office, McMahan Hall** ⑤ **free** ♿ **yes**

Gallaudet University
(4, D11) Gallaudet is the world's only accredited liberal arts college for the deaf. Founded in 1857 as a primary school, it became a college in 1864. In the sports world, it's known as the home of the huddle, invented in 1894 so football players could signal their plays while safe from prying eyes.
✉ **800 Florida Ave NE** ☎ **651-5505,** TDD 651-5359 🅴 **www.gallaudet.edu** 🚌 **90, 92, 93** ⊘ **tours Mon-Fri 10am & 1pm** ⑤ **free** ♿ **yes**

George Washington University (5, D2)
In 1821, Congress chartered GWU as a secular institution, with a prohibition against religious discrimination toward students or teachers. In 1912, the school began migrating from Downtown to Foggy Bottom. The dull campus is known for shows at the Lisner Auditorium. Famous alumns include J Edgar Hoover and Colin Powell.
✉ **803 22nd St NW** ☎ **994-1000** 🅴 **www.gwu.edu** Ⓜ **Foggy Bottom/GWU** ⊘ **Mon-Fri 9am-5pm** ⑤ **free** ♿ **yes**

Georgetown University (4, C3)
Maryland was founded as a Roman Catholic colony, so it's not surprising that the first Catholic college in America started here in 1789. Today, Georgetown is best known for three things: its Hoyas basketball team (from *hoya saxa,* Latin for 'what rocks'), for alumnus William Jefferson Clinton and for the steps at 36th & Prospect, which were featured in *The Exorcist.*
✉ **37th & O Sts NW** ☎ **687-6583** 🅴 **www.georgetown.edu** Ⓜ **Foggy Bottom/GWU** 🚌 **D2, D4, G2** ⊘ **tours Mon-Sat; call for hrs** ⑤ **free** ♿ **yes**

Howard University
(4, B9) Founded in 1867 to educate African Americans freed after the Civil War, Howard has produced generations of leaders, from Ralph Bunche and Edward Brooke to Thurgood Marshall and Vernon Jordan, plus artists and writers including Toni Morrison and Imamu Amiri Baraka.
✉ **2400 6th St NW** ☎ **806-6100, tour reservations 806-2900** 🅴 **www.howard.edu** Ⓜ **Shaw/Howard, U St/Cardozo** 🚌 **70, 71, G2** ⊘ **tours Mon-Fri 10am, noon & 2pm when school's in session (reservations required)** ⑤ **free** ♿ **yes**

Howard University, intellectual focal point of the Shaw District

QUIRKY WASHINGTON

In a city devoted to not making waves, there are still a few sights that can raise an eyebrow.

Counter Counter Spy International (5, C5)
It's Spy vs Spy vs Spy at CCS International, the security supplies boutique where you can buy simple stuff like a briefcase with a solid lock or not-so-simple stuff like equipment to make sure that no one is tapping your phone line.
✉ **1027 Connecticut Ave NW** ☎ **887-1717, 800-916-9227** Ⓜ Farragut North ⏱ Mon-Fri 9am-6pm, Sat 10am-3pm ⑤ free ♿ yes

The Mansion on O St (5, A3) When is a B&B not a B&B? When it charges $5 to see its 17 rooms, and when each room is wildly different, done up like a log cabin or accessorized with an aquarium headboard. Part gallery, part private club, it's completely idiosyncratic. See money and imagination either wreak utter havoc or take flight, depending on your point of view.
✉ **2020 O St NW** ☎ **496-2000** ⓔ www.erols.com/mansion Ⓜ Dupont Circle ⏱ call ahead or take your chances ⑤ $5

National Museum of Health & Medicine (6, D6) This museum's self-described role as 'an element of the Armed Forces Pathology Unit' really says it all. Formerly the Army Medical Museum, this has become the place to see the bullet that killed Lincoln and the amputated leg of General Daniel Sickles (the general used to visit on the anniversary of his and his leg's separation). View live leeches, dead smokers' lungs and other cool stuff.
✉ **Bldg 54, Walter Reed Army Medical Center, 6900 Georgia Ave NW** ☎ **782-2200** ⓔ www.natmedmuse.afip.org Ⓜ Takoma 🚌 52, 53, 54 📷 photo ID required to drive onto WRAMC ⏱ 10am-5:30pm ⑤ free ♿ yes

Political Americana (5, E14) If you've managed to lose your Clinton-Gore button (or worse yet, your Dole-Kemp bumper stickers), don't give up hope quite yet. The folks at Political Americana carry specimens of just about all political memorabilia produced in the last 100 years, regardless of taste.
✉ **Union Station, 50 Massachusetts Ave NE (also at the National Gallery)** ☎ **547-1685** ⓔ www.politicalamericana.com Ⓜ Union Station ⏱ Mon-Sat 10am-9pm, Sun noon-6pm ⑤ free ♿ yes

Scottish Rite Temple (4, C7) The US headquarters for the Masons (whose illustrious past members have included such luminaries as George Washington and J Edgar Hoover), this grand Greco-Franco temple is splendid to walk around, just to see the lions, the doors and the mosaic work. Visitors can take the guided tour through the building interior and learn what the images mean and (quite literally) how they all add up.
✉ **1733 16th St NW** ☎ **232-3579** Ⓜ Dupont Circle 🚌 S2 ⏱ Mon-Fri 8am-4pm ⑤ free ♿ yes

Thursday Night Roller Hockey (5, D5) People have been in-line skating on Pennsylvania Ave right in front of the White House ever since the street was closed for security reasons during the Clinton administration. Nowadays, an informal roller-hockey league plays here every Thursday night (at least during the school year).
✉ **1600 Pennsylvania Ave NW** Ⓜ McPherson Sq ⏱ Thurs evening ⑤ free ♿ yes

Wet (4, G10) Go-go boys dancing on top of the bar and under the showers here draw men and their straight women friends to the nasty heart of Southeast DC. Unlike their counterparts at places like Splash in New York City, these guys strip down to their socks.
✉ **52 L St SE** ☎ **488-1200** Ⓜ Navy Yard ⏱ 8pm-2am (Fri-Sat to 3am); shows at 9pm ⑤ $3 ($7 after 9pm)

WASHINGTON FOR CHILDREN

From school field trips to summer vacations with Mom and Dad, Washington has always been a destination for children. There isn't an attraction in town that doesn't anticipate kids – even if it's child-wary (the Phillips Collection makes a gentle request that you hold your child's hand). Most major attractions are geared for families, offering special children's guides, strollers and snack bars with kid-friendly food.

Capital Children's Museum (5, C15)

A 25-year-old experiment in exploration, this museum features interactive exhibits that encourage kids to touch, feel, taste and smell. ✉ 800 3d St NE ☎ 675-4120 e www.ccm.org Ⓜ Union Station 🅿 hourly parking at Union Station ⏱ Tues-Sun 10am-5pm (also open on Mon holidays, the Mon after Easter, the Mon btw Dec 25 & Jan 1) $ $7/5, children 2 & under free; half-price Sun before noon ♿ yes

Federal Bureau of Investigation (5, E9)

A half-million people visit the FBI every year, including countless families with children who are enthralled with the walk-through of the FBI laboratory and thrilled by the sharpshooting at the firing range that closes the hourlong tour. To secure your spot on a tour, call ahead; Americans can

Kalorama tree-bonding

Rick Gerharter

also reserve tickets through their congressional representatives. ✉ J Edgar Hoover Bldg, 935 Pennsylvania Ave NW ☎ 324-3447 e www.fbi.gov Ⓜ Archives/Navy Memorial, Federal Center, Metro Center ⏱ Mon-Fri 8:45am-4:15pm (tour line may close early during peak times) $ free ♿ yes

Kalorama Playground (3, D1)

This spot in Kalorama Park boasts almost everything a city playground can hope for – a convenient location near the center of Adams-Morgan, a separate tot lot, serious playground equipment for older kids and a view of the city for parents. ✉ Columbia Rd & Kalorama Rd NW ☎ 673-7606 Ⓜ Dupont Circle 🚌 42, L2 ⏱ sunrise-sunset $ free ♿ yes

National Bureau of Printing & Engraving (5, H7)

Who can resist the spectacle of pages and pages of money coming off the presses at 8000 sheets an hour? Tours take 30 minutes; free timed-entry tickets are available on a first-come, first-served basis at the ticket office from Apr through Sept, so come early. ✉ 14th & C Sts SW ☎ 874-3019 e www.moneyfactory.com Ⓜ Smithsonian ⏱ Mon-Fri 9am-2pm $ free ♿ yes

National Geographic Explorers Hall (5, B5)

The people who brought us the much-beloved *National Geographic* magazine take kids to the far corners of the globe in Explorers Hall, where a recent exhibit

More Kid Stuff

Other particularly kid-friendly attractions covered elsewhere in the book include **Blazing Saddles** (p. 46), the **National Gallery of Art** (p. 21), the **National Theatre** (p. 91), the **National Air and Space Museum** (p. 20), the **Washington Chamber Symphony** (p. 93) and **Wolf Trap Farm for Performing Arts** (p. 93).

focused on a 15-month walk across the Sahara. 'Passport Fridays' feature such special events as performances of African music and wildlife appearances.
✉ 17th & M Sts NW ☎ 857-7588 🄴 www .nationalgeographic .com 🄼 Farragut North ⏰ Mon-Sat 9am-5pm, Sun 10am-5pm ⑤ free ♿ yes

National Postal Museum (5, D13)
Don't worry – your kids won't get bored looking at a bunch of stamps, though there are lots. There's plenty more: interactive exhibits on direct mail and 'Moving the Mail,' a show that features the planes, trains and automobiles that bring us the mail, just for starters.
✉ Massachusetts Ave btw 1st & N Capitol Sts NE ☎ 357-2991 🄴 www.si.edu/postal 🄼 Union Station ⏰ 10am-5:30pm ⑤ free ♿ yes

Newseum (4, E4)
This kid-friendly monument to freedom of the press includes lively conventional exhibits like the News History Wall and the Berlin Wall section, plus interactive exhibits where kids can try their hands at TV broadcasting and test their skills as newspaper reporters or photojournalists.
✉ 1101 Wilson Blvd, Arlington, VA ☎ 703-284-3544 🄴 www .newseum.org 🄼 Rosslyn ⏰ Tues-Sun 10am-5pm ⑤ free ♿ yes

Smithsonian Discovery Theater
(5, H8) Tucked inside the Arts & Industries Building

lies a repertory theater for children. Three- to seven-year-olds can see The Wizard of Oz; there's also a musical about Satchel Paige and the Negro League ballplayers for ages five to nine and a salsa version of A Comedy of Errors for the eight-to-16 set.
✉ 900 Jefferson Dr SW ☎ 357-1500 🄴 www .discoverytheater.si.edu 🄼 Smithsonian, L'Enfant Plaza ⏰ box office Mon-Fri 9am-5pm, performances Mon-Sat 10 & 11:30am & 1:30pm (times may vary) ⑤ $5 ♿ yes

US Naval Observatory (4, B4)
Every Monday night, big people and small people line up for the 90min tour to talk to the astronomers, look through the telescopes and check out the Master Clock for the whole

USA. The vice president's residence, on the grounds above the Massachusetts Ave entrance, is not part of the tour, but you can peek at the outside.
✉ 3450 Massachusetts Ave NW ☎ 762-1438 🚍 N2, N3, N4, N6, N7 ⏰ Mon 8:30pm except holidays ⑤ free

Washington Doll's House & Toy Museum (6, D4)
This exceptional collection of Victorian dollhouses and toys includes a tiny Capitol Building, miniature castles and other flights of fancy. The gift shop, with dolls, accessories and dollhouse kits, may be as interesting as the collection itself.
✉ 5236 44th St NW ☎ 244-0024 🄼 Friendship Hts 🚍 30, 32, 34, 35, 36 ⏰ Mon-Sat 10am-5pm ⑤ $4/2

Babysitting
Many hotels provide babysitting services. Ask at the front desk for help. You can also call **WeeSit** (☎ 703-764-1542), which charges $12-13/hr, with a four-hour minimum, a $12 transportation charge and a supplemental cost for additional siblings. You can also call **White House Nannies** (☎ 301-652-8808, 800-270-6266), which charges $12-15/hr and a small agency fee. Advance bookings are always a good idea.

Rick Gerharter

KEEPING FIT

With all the parks, all the students and all the twenty- and thirtysomethings doing an internship in Congress, it's not surprising to see people in sweats or shorts everywhere.

Runners dot the Mall, the parks and the streets. An enormous network of bike trails runs from Capitol Hill and the waterfront up Rock Creek Park deep into Maryland, and over the bridges and down past Mount Vernon. In poor weather, gym crowds reach critical mass. Suffice to say, if physical training is part of your regimen, you'll have no excuses for backsliding when you visit DC.

Blazing Saddles
(5, E8) Rent one of five types of bikes for adults and kids to explore the Mall and monuments. At the Metro Center store, you'll get a map outlining five favorite bike routes, complete with directions ('turn right in 1.2 miles, then go .3 miles...') to help you keep your bearings.
✉ 445 11th St NW
☎ 544-0055 @ www .blazingsaddles.com

Ⓜ Metro Center
🕐 9am-7pm
$ $7-11/hr (2hr minimum), $28-48/day

East Potomac Golf Course
(4, H8) You can play a full 18 holes of golf, practice your swing at the driving range or wage a Quixotic battle with the windmills at the miniature golf course, all within view of the water, the major monuments and National Airport.
✉ 972 Ohio Dr SW
☎ 554-7660
@ www.golfdc.com
Ⓜ Smithsonian
🕐 sunrise-sunset (driving range to 9pm), mini golf Apr-Oct Sat-Sun
$ 9 holes Mon-Fri $11, Sat-Sun $14; 18 holes Mon-Fri $16.50, Sat-Sun $22; mini golf $4.50/round

Results the Gym
(4, B8) Not everyone here is a gay man under 40, but there are times of the day (say, 6pm on Monday) when it feels that way. The stylish, spotless facilities host classes for every taste, from ab workouts and aerobics to yoga and bodypump, for no extra charge.
✉ 1612 U St NW
☎ 518-0001 Ⓜ U St/ Cardozo, Dupont Circle
🚌 90, 92, 93, 96, 98, S1, S2, S4 🕐 Mon-Fri 5:30am-11pm, Sat-Sun 9am-8pm $ $20/day
♿ yes

Rock Creek Park Golf Course
(6, D5) The 18 holes here range up and down the hills and dales of Northwest Washington. It's a great getaway from the city

Crisp air and fall foliage render running a breeze in DC.

Rick Gerharter

right in the middle of town.
✉ **1600 Rittenhouse St NW** ☎ 882-7332
🚌 S1, S2, S4 🚗 enter from Beach Dr south of Military Rd or Rittenhouse St west of 16th St ⏰ Apr-Oct 6am-9pm, Nov-Mar 7am-5:30pm 💲 9 holes Mon-Fri $9, Sat-Sun $12.20; 18 holes Mon-Fri $15, Sat-Sun $19 ♿ yes

Rock Creek Park Horse Center (6, D5)
Jackie Kennedy used to ride her horses in real horse country around Middleburg, Virginia, but you can take a 1hr guided ride or treat a child to a pony ride right here in Rock Creek Park.
✉ **5100 Glover Rd NW at Military Rd** ☎ 362-0117 🚌 E2, E3, E4 ⏰ Tues-Thurs 3pm, Sat-Sun noon, 1:30 & 3pm (reservations required) 💲 guided ride about $21/hr, 15min pony ride $7.50

Yakkin' on the Potomac

SpiralFlight (2, A1)
If you don't care for the selection of yoga classes at the gym on the corner nearest you, you could try this 'center for yoga and the arts.' It's dedicated to, well, yoga as well as tai chi and the like.
✉ **1726 Wisconsin Ave NW** ☎ 965-1645

🚌 30, 32, 34, 35, 36 ⏰ hrs vary 💲 $13

Tidal Basin Boathouse (5, J6)
You can rent paddleboats year-round from the boathouse across from the Jefferson Memorial. Feel the romance any time of the year, but particularly when the cherry trees are in bloom.
✉ **East Basin Dr & Raoul Wallenberg Pl (15th St) SW** ☎ 479-2426 Ⓜ Smithsonian ⏰ Mon-Fri 10am-6pm, Sat-Sun 10am-7pm 💲 $7/hr (2-seater), $14/hr (4-seater)

Thompson Boat Center (4, D5)
This modest, modern boathouse, hidden under an overpass where Rock Creek and the C&O Canal meet the Potomac, rents canoes, kayaks, rowing shells and Sunfish. Landlubbers can snag bikes to cruise the city or the C&O towpath.
✉ **2900 Virginia Ave NW** ☎ 333-9543 🅴 www.guestservices.com/tbc Ⓜ Foggy Bottom/GWU ⏰ Mon-Sat 6am-8pm,

Exercise means different things for different folks.

Sun 7am-7pm 💲 watercraft $8-13/hr, $22-30/day; bikes $4-8/hr, $14-25/day ♿ fair

YWCA (5, D9)
This fitness center for men and women right in the center of Downtown features exercise studios, free weights, machines and a 25m swimming pool. Yoga, Pilates and aerobics classes are available at no extra charge.
✉ **624 9th St NW** ☎ 626-0710 🅴 www.ywcanca.org Ⓜ Gallery Pl/Chinatown ⏰ Mon-Fri 6:30am-9pm, Sat 8:30am-4:30pm, Sun 10am-4:30pm 💲 $12/day ♿ yes

Washington Tennis Center (6, D5)
Ten hard courts and 15 clay courts sit on the east edge of Rock Creek Park near the Carter Barron Amphitheater. Five of the hard courts are for cold-weather play. Call the pro shop for reservations.
✉ **16th & Kennedy Sts NW** ☎ 722-5949 🚌 S1, S2, S4 ⏰ 7am-11pm 💲 $3.25-28/hr ♿ yes

out & about

WALKING TOURS
Alexandria

From the King St Metro station, head up to King St, then turn right, toward the Potomac. Look back at the George Washington Masonic National Memorial **1**, across the tracks. Walk to Washington St, grabbing a snack on the way at Lite Fair **2**. Turn right on Washington and go one block to the Lyceum **3**, at Prince St; it houses a local history museum. Double back to King St and continue toward the river past the visitors' center **4**, at the corner of Fairfax St, to the Torpedo Factory Art Center **5**, at the foot of the street. Go through the Torpedo Factory to the Alexandria Seaport Center **6**, at the foot of Cameron St, and head up Cameron past the Carlyle House **7** and Gadsby's Tavern **8**, on Royal St between Cameron and King. Turn right on Pitt St to Oronoco St, then left and go two blocks to N Washington St. Turn left again on Washington and head back to Christ Church **9**, at Cameron St. Explore the church and the church-

yard, exiting on Columbus. Turn left on Columbus, get to King, and head back to the Metro. Hungry again? Stop at the Majestic Cafe **10** along the way.

George Washington Masonic National
   Monument (p. 38)
Lite Fair (p. 75)
Torpedo Factory Art Center (p. 36)
Majestic Cafe (p. 75)

Getting creative at the Torpedo Factory

Rick Gerharter

distance 3 miles (4km) duration 4hrs
▶ start **M** King St Metro
● end **M** King St Metro

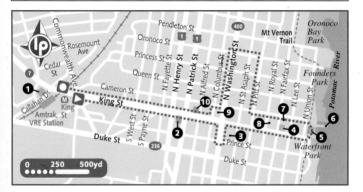

Capitol Hill

From the Eastern Market Metro station, head west on Pennsylvania Ave a short block to 7th St SE, turn right on 7th and go one block north to Eastern Market ❶, where you can eat at the Market Lunch café if you're patient or early. Roam through the market, then continue up 7th to E Capitol St. Turn left to the Capitol, passing the Folger Shakespeare Library ❷, Library of Congress ❸ and Supreme Court ❹ on the way. Go around the Capitol's north side ❺ to the West Front ❻,

Royo's 'After Joan Miró,' National Gallery

overlooking the Mall. Walk around the pool to Madison Dr, continuing west past the National Gallery ❼. Cross 7th St NW and turn left; head across the Mall to the Hirshhorn Museum and Sculpture Garden ❽, along Jefferson Dr. Follow Jefferson past the Arts & Industries Building ❾ and the Castle ❿ to the Smithsonian Metro station.

distance 1.5 miles (2km) **duration** 2hrs
▶ **start** Ⓜ Eastern Market Metro
● **end** Ⓜ Smithsonian Metro

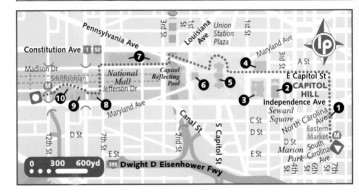

New U St

From the corner of 13th and U Sts, head east on the north side of U St past the Lincoln Theater ❶ (Washington's answer to the Apollo in New York City) and Ben's Chili Bowl ❷ (best place in the District for a burger or a dog), to Vermont Ave and the African American Civil War Memorial ❸. Turn right on Vermont and head south to S St, where you turn left and go one block to 10th St. Turn right and proceed one full block to R; turn right again and head west past the churches ❹ on the far side of

SIGHTS & HIGHLIGHTS

Ben's Chili Bowl (p. 85)
African American Civil War
  Memorial (p. 38)
Republic Gardens (p. 89)

Monuments to the courage to fight...

Rick Gerharter

distance 2 miles (3km)
duration 3hrs
▶ start 13th & U Sts
● end 13th & U Sts

Vermont to 13th St. Turn right, and head north to T St, passing the Whitelaw Apartments ❺, which was the finest African American hotel in the city during the dark days of 'Jim Crow' segregation laws. Turn left on T St and head to 14th St, past the old post office ❻, which was one of the first to hire African American postal workers. Turn right on U St and head back to the Metro station, passing the nightspot Republic Gardens ❼ along the way.

Northwest Ramble

From the U St/Cardozo Metro, head west along the south side of U St to 18th St, past Results the Gym ❶ and the Chi-Cha Lounge ❷. Watch the neighborhood change block by block. Turn left on 17th St and head south to Q St. Turn right on Q, past Kramerbooks and its Afterwords

...and to the courage not to fight

SIGHTS & HIGHLIGHTS

Results the Gym (p. 46)
Chi-Cha Lounge (p. 88)
Kramerbooks and Afterwords
   café (p. 62)
Phillips Collection (p. 35)
Dumbarton Oaks (p. 37)

café ❸ on 19th St. Continue west past the Indian Embassy, with the statue of Gandhi ❹, and the Phillips Collection ❺ over Rock Creek and into Georgetown. Turn right on 31st St, passing Tudor Place ❻. Turn left on R St, pass the entrance to Dumbarton Oaks ❼ and continue to Wisconsin Ave. Turn left on Wisconsin and head down the hill past the hotels and shops to the corner of M St NW, the heart of Georgetown.

distance 3 miles (4km) **duration** 4hrs
▶ **start** Ⓜ U St/Cardozo Metro
● **end** Wisconsin Ave & M St

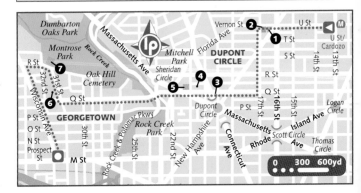

EXCURSIONS
Annapolis   (1, B4)

Annapolis is a living, breathing city that could pass for a theme park on 18th-century American life. Founded in 1649, it prospered on the triangular trade among England, America and the English colonies in the West Indies. It became capital of the colony of Maryland in 1695 and served briefly as the capital of the US in 1783.

INFORMATION

30 miles (48km) east of Washington, DC

🚋 New York Ave east to Hwy 50

☎ 410-280-0445

ⓔ www.visit-annapolis.org

ⓘ visitors' center 26 West St

⊘ visitors' center 9am-5pm

✕ McGarvey's Saloon and Oyster Bar (8 Market Space; ☎ 410-263-5700)

Today, the center of town is filled with the largest concentration of Georgian buildings in the country. The **Maryland State House**, built in 1788, and **St Anne's Episcopal Church** dominate the skyline. You'll find all sorts of mariners on the city streets, from midshipmen attending the US Naval Academy (on the east end of the city center) to civilian sailors at the marinas and sailing schools elsewhere on the waterfront.

Civilian students go to **St John's College**, just north of the city center. The third-oldest college in the country, it's known for its 'Great Books' curriculum. If you feel like a little more driving, wander the backroads south from the city and explore the west shore of Chesapeake Bay down to **Point Lookout**, 100 miles (160km) away, or cross the Chesapeake Bay Bridge and tour the Eastern Shore, lined with farms and fishing towns all the way down to the Virginia state line.

The State House gardens: captivating year round, deadly during pollen season

Mount Vernon   (1, C3)

Americans have seen images of the white house with the red roof for generations, and American homebuilders have thrown up bad copies from coast to coast, so it's hard to appreciate either the beauty of the site or the beauty of George Washington's work until you find yourself on the most famous front porch in the country, looking over the Potomac.

Washington wrote that 'no estate in the United States is more pleasantly situated,' and it's hard to argue as one drives down the parkway from the capital through the lush green woods that line the river. As you enter the grounds, an enormous bowling green stretches before you, with the main house at the end. A kitchen garden hides behind the hedges on one side of the lawn, a pleasure garden behind the hedges on the other. Beautifully restored outbuildings, from the kitchen and the smokehouse to the slave quarters, complete the picture of a working 18th-century plantation.

INFORMATION

- *16 miles (26km) south of Washington, DC*
- Ⓜ Huntington station; transfer to Fairfax Connector bus No 101 (50¢) to Mount Vernon
- 🚘 I-66 or I-395 across the Potomac to George Washington Memorial Pkwy (Route 400) south to Mount Vernon
- ☎ 703-780-2000
- ⓔ www.mountvernon.org
- ⓘ information center at entrance to estate
- ◷ Apr-Aug 8am-5pm; Mar, Sept & Oct 9am-5pm; Nov-Feb 9am-4pm
- Ⓢ $9/8.50/4.50; audio guide $3
- ✕ Mount Vernon Inn (☎ 703-780-0011)

Inside, the rooms are painted and furnished in their original styles. Many of the furnishings actually date from the Washingtons' time. The guides from the Mount Vernon Ladies Association (which has owned the estate since 1858) will show you through the public rooms and the private rooms on the 2nd floor, including the bedroom where Washington died.

Unable to Beat a Retreat

Perhaps no US president has spent as much time trying to avoid the limelight – *before* being elected – as George Washington. Upon his victory over the British in 1783, he tried to retire to his estate, desiring nothing more than the relaxed life of a country farmer. The Continental Congress would have none of that, though, and they brought him in as a leader in 1787. A year later, under the new Constitution, Washington was elected president.

Believing his work done after one term, Washington again attempted retirement. However, the Electoral College mandated him into office for another four years. Even after his second term, Washington was denied peace, reluctantly accepting charge of US troops when the French threatened in 1798. He died soon afterward, having enjoyed retirement at Mt Vernon for only one year.

– *Vivek Waglé*

Rehoboth Beach   (1, C5)

Rehoboth, Delaware, and its ugly sister of Ocean City, Maryland, are the spots where Washington goes to the shore. They're a long ways away – around three hours or more if there's an accident on the Chesapeake Bay Bridge, but they're as close as you can get to the ocean, and the town and its surroundings are worth the trek once you're there.

The town itself verges on, but does not descend into, the quaint. It's an old religious summer camp from the 1870s that grew into a middle-class summer resort at the turn of the last century. Its cottages slept peacefully until the 1970s, when it began drawing gay and lesbian vacationers from DC and Philadelphia. These new visitors brought a broader mix of other summer people who were drawn by the small town's charm and the beautiful natural setting.

Just north of Rehoboth, where Delaware Bay empties into the ocean, **Cape Henlopen State Park** features woods and campgrounds and 5 miles (8km) of shoreline. Just south of town, the **Delaware Shores State Park** protects the 7-mile-long (11km) isthmus between the ocean and Rehoboth Bay.

INFORMATION

120 miles (190km) southeast of Washington, DC

- New York Ave east to Hwy 50, past Annapolis and over Chesapeake Bay to Route 404 east to Route 1 south to Rehoboth
- ☎ 302-227-2233, 800-441-1329
- e www.rehoboth.com
- ① visitors' center (501 Rehoboth Ave)
- ② visitors' center Mon-Fri 9am-5pm, Sat-Sun 9am-1pm
- ✕ Blue Moon Restaurant (35 Baltimore Ave; ☎ 302-227-6515)

Happy Clam Hunting

Clam digging is a favorite, and productive, pastime of Rehoboth beachgoers. Before you go digging, you might want to consult with a bait shop or check at the state parks for maps that tell you where the bountiful clam beds are. Next, get a plastic beach bucket, or wear shorts or a swimsuit with big pockets, and head for Rehoboth Bay at low tide. Try to find a place where the water is about 2ft deep and the bottom is a composite of mud and sand.

When you're in a spot where the bottom has a silty texture, bend over and dig your fingers into the bottom to a depth of about your middle knuckles. Then begin squeezing your fingers together with your thumbs as though you're kneading bread dough.

Start close to your feet and explore the bottom in quadrants within a radius of 2ft around you. When you find a clam, it may try to burrow away – hang on! It's likely to be part of a colony, so don't lose your spot. After you've caught it, put it in your pocket or bucket and keep hunting until your pockets are full. Most people will eat six to 12 clams, so harvest accordingly. Those with stalwart immune systems can enjoy the shellfish raw or steamed.

– Laura Harger & Vivek Waglé

Shenandoah National Park   (1, C3)

On a clear day, the line of the Blue Ridge Mountains beckons from Dulles Airport, prompting nature lovers to hop in their cars and make the two-hour drive to the ridgeline (a longer trip during peak hours). You'll find thick hardwood forests that open up suddenly to views of the Shenandoah Valley, thousands of feet below. Look closer and you'll discover hundreds of miles of trails, including 101 miles (162km) of the Appalachian Trail itself, and scores of campgrounds and picnic sites. Numerous streams tumble down

INFORMATION

90 miles (145km) west of Washington, DC

🚗 I-66 west to Hwy 340 at Front Royal; south on Hwy 340 to park entrance at north end of Skyline Dr; south on Skyline Dr to Hwy 211 east to I-66 east to DC

☎ 540-999-3500

e www.nps.gov/shen

ⓘ Dickey Ridge Visitor Center (Mile 4.6 on Skyline Dr)

🕐 visitors' center Apr-Nov 8:30am-5pm

$ $5/person, $10/car (no extra charge for occupants)

✕ Skyline Restaurant (Mile 42.5 on Skyline Dr; ☎ 540-999-2211)

Milling around in the duck pond

the mountains, and wildlife wanders through the woods.

It's a stunning view anytime, most of all when the leaves turn in the fall and almost every other person in Greater Washington is on the road with you. The park's open year round, though Skyline Dr (the main attraction) might close in bad weather.

If you take the loop from DC to Front Royal, up to Skyline Dr and back down at Thornton Gap, you'll pass through Virginia hunt country. Jackie Kennedy kept a place near Middleburg when she lived in the White House. In Washington, Virginia, the Inn at Little Washington (309 Middle St; ☎ 540-675-3800) draws DC gourmands, who plan months in advance for a trip here.

ORGANIZED TOURS

Bike the Sites (5, G8)
These 3hr tours cover 55 sights in the city without leaving the bike paths. Bike rental and helmets and snacks are included. Custom tours are also available.
✉ **12th St & Jefferson Dr SW** ☎ **966-8662** ◷ May-Nov 10am (& 2pm for overflow) ⓢ $40/30

C&O Canal Barge Rides (2, D4)
Mule-drawn canal boats ply the waters between Georgetown and Great Falls, about 6 miles (10km) upstream.
✉ **1057 Thomas Jefferson St NW** ☎ **653-5190** ◷ Apr-May: Thurs-Fri 11am, 3pm; Sat-Sun 11am, 1:30pm, 3pm; June-Aug: Wed-Sun 11am, 1:30pm, 3pm; Sept-Oct: Thurs-Fri 11am, 3pm; Sat-Sun 11am, 1:30pm, 3pm ⓢ $8/6/5

Duck Tours (5, E14)
Tired of buses? Take a narrated tour of the monuments on a WWII amphibious landing craft. Start on dry land and run through the middle of the Potomac.
✉ **Union Station, 50 Massachusetts Ave NE** ☎ **996-3825** ◷ Apr-Oct hourly 10am-3pm ⓢ $24/12

Potomac Riverboat Company (6, J5)
Visit Mount Vernon by boat from Alexandria or enjoy a longish cruise between Alexandria and the Georgetown dock.
✉ **Alexandria Dock, foot of King St, Alexandria, VA** ☎ **703-548-9000** ◷ May-Sept Tues-Sat 11:30am-9:30pm, Sun 11:30am-7:30pm; Apr & Oct Sat-Sun 11:30am-5:30pm ⓢ $5-26

Scandal Tour (5, F8)
In this 90min stroll through Washington history, costumed actors enact stories from political scandals.
✉ **meet at Old Post Office Pavilion, 12th St NW** ☎ **783-7212** ◷ Sat 1pm ⓢ $30

Tour DC
Veteran travel writer Mary Kay Ricks leads walking tours of various Washington neighborhoods from Georgetown to Dupont Circle.
✉ **meet at Metro stations** ☎ **301-588-8999** ◷ hrs vary ⓢ $12-18

Tourmobile Sightseeing (5, E14)
The American Heritage Tour trams make 25 stops around town during this tour. Alternatively, tour Mount Vernon or the Frederick Douglass Home at Cedar Hill.
✉ **ticket booths at Union Station, White House Information Center & Washington Monument** ☎ **554-5100** ◷ Jun 15-Labor Day 9:30am-6:30pm, Labor Day-Jun 14 9:30am-4:30pm ⓢ **American Heritage Tour $18/8**

The canal's immediate obsolescence is just water under the bridge these days.

Rick Gerharter

shopping

Not many people go to Washington to go shopping, unless they're shopping for power and influence. To start, there's no central shopping district. Like most American city centers, Downtown Washington was in trouble in the 1960s, even before the '68 riots burned out the commercial strips along 14th St NW and elsewhere. Garfinckel's, Woodword & Lothrop and the other department stores that lined F and G Sts closed years ago. There is a small Hecht's at 12th St and G NW, but it's the only significant store around aside from some drugstores, a couple of good bookstores and the new strip of boutiques along 7th St NW.

Shop Around the Clock

If you have an emergency or you're on your way home from a club, you can fill a prescription or buy some sunglasses at one of the 24-hour **CVS** pharmacies (p. 119). You can get something to eat or something to read until 1am weeknights and around the clock on weekends at **Kramerbooks** (see p. 62), with a cafe on site. Otherwise, plan on shopping or refueling before 11pm or midnight, unless your hotel happens to have 24-hour room service.

To make matters worse, there's no tradition of shopping here. Until the Reagan years, even people with money didn't throw their money around on stuff that showed. Consumption is more conspicuous these days, but there's still a natural conservatism to Washington life that keeps shoppers hugging the middle of the road.

Shopping Districts

What shopping there is in the District is almost entirely situated west of 14th St NW, from the south fringes of the **Dupont Circle** area (offering books, music and arty stuff) to the north end of **Adams-Morgan** (clothes, music and ethnic trinkets), and farther west across Rock Creek Park. Trendy **Georgetown** features everything from antique stores to a Staples office supply center to a small, upscale mall. **Friendship Heights**, up north, straddling the Maryland state line, boasts two smallish shopping centers as well as freestanding stores such as Tiffany, Versace and Saks Fifth Avenue. In the Downtown area, you can do some casual browsing in the new **Penn Quarter** along 7th St NW, a fledgling entertainment district featuring a string of galleries and restaurants. However, if you're looking for some serious shopping, you have to travel out to Virginia, which offers a number of big-ticket areas – **Pentagon City** (two malls to serve you), **Tysons Corner** (two huge malls and lots of little ones) and **Old Town** in Alexandria (boutique heaven).

Fishy freshness at the Seafood Market

DEPARTMENT STORES & MALLS

Fashion Centre at Pentagon City (4, J4)

Only 14 minutes by train from Metro Center, this is where lots of office workers in Washington come to shop. Four levels of shops include Macy's, Nordstrom, the Disney Store and Sunglass Hut, plus a few local operations to give you a hint that you're in Virginia.

✉ 1110 S Hayes St, Arlington, VA ☎ 703-415-2400 Ⓜ Pentagon City ◷ Mon-Sat 10am-9:30pm, Sun 11am-6pm

Filene's Basement (5, B4)

You might find a real deal among the men's and women's clothes and accessories in this discount operation. Then again, you might not. Nothing ventured, nothing gained.

✉ 1133 Connecticut Ave NW ☎ 872-8430 Ⓜ Farragut North ◷ Mon-Sat 9:30am-8pm, Sun noon-5pm

Georgetown Park Mall (2, D2)

The largest shopping mall inside DC has rounded up the usual suspects: J Crew, Abercrombie & Fitch and Ralph Lauren. You'll find typical fast-food fare at the food court, but classier eats, in the form of Dean & DeLuca, wait

Don't forget to top off your shopping stylishly.

Rick Gerharter

outside the west entrance on M St.

✉ 3222 M St NW ☎ 298-5577 Ⓜ Foggy Bottom/GWU 🚌 30, 32, 34, 35, 36, Georgetown shuttles ◷ Mon-Sat 10am-9pm, Sun noon-6pm

Hecht's (5, D8)

The only surviving department store in Downtown DC, Hecht's deserves an honorable mention for sheer endurance. The place carries nothing you won't find in any basic US department store, but it's a good stop for everyday items.

✉ 12th & G Sts NW ☎ 628-6661 Ⓜ Metro

Center ◷ Mon-Sat 10am-8pm, Sun noon-6pm

Neiman-Marcus (6, D4)

When you're looking for something flashy or edgy or just plain expensive, head here, but be sure to take your American Express card or your checkbook because Neiman's doesn't accept Visa or MasterCard as normal stores do.

✉ Mazza Gallerie, 5300 Wisconsin Ave NW ☎ 966-9700 Ⓜ Friendship Hts ◷ Mon-Fri 10am-8pm, Sat 10am-7pm, Sun noon-6pm

Mazza Gallerie (6, D4)

The toniest little mall in the District features Neiman's, the Saks men's store and a posh multiplex on the top floor. There's also a Filene's Basement, a Foot Locker and other less rarified institutions to add to the mix.

✉ 5300 Wisconsin Ave NW ☎ 966-6114

Tax Tips

The sales tax in the District is 5.75%. Maryland charges 5%, and Virginia charges 4% on food and 4.5% on everything else. If you have your purchase shipped out of the area or out of the country, most retailers will not charge sales tax unless they have a branch location in the US state where the goods are heading.

🅜 Friendship Hts
🕐 Mon-Fri 10am-8pm,
Sat 10am-6pm, Sun
noon-5pm

Nordstrom (4, J4)
You'll find a good selection
of attractive, if unchalleng-
ing, clothes and shoes,
with the service you'd find
in a good shoe store.
✉ Fashion Centre at
Pentagon City ☎ 703-
415-1121 🅜 Pentagon
City 🕐 Mon-Sat 10am-
9:30pm, Sun 11am-6pm

Potomac Mills (1, C3)
The queen of the outlet
malls in the Washington
area contains over 200 outlets, from Big Dog to Ikea to
Ann Taylor. It's a trek to get
there and a trek when you
get there, but the crowds
keep coming anyway.
✉ 2700 Potomac Mills
Circle, Prince William,
VA ☎ 703-643-1770
🚌 15 miles (24km)
south of Capital
Beltway on I-95
🕐 Mon-Fri 10am-
9:30pm, Sat 9:30am-
9:30pm, Sun 10am-7pm

Saks Fifth Avenue
(6, D4) Shop for the best
high-end men's clothes in
town and upscale women's
wear that ranges from cos-
metics to couture to power
suits for working moms.
The men's store is on the
ground floor of Mazza
Gallerie. The freestanding
main store is two blocks
north, over the Maryland
line in Chevy Chase.
✉ 5555 Wisconsin Ave
NW, Chevy Chase, MD
☎ 301-657-9000
🅜 Friendship Hts
🕐 Mon-Sat 10am-6pm
(Thurs to 9pm), Sun
noon-6pm

Tysons Corner Center
(6, F1) Fifty years ago, a
gas station marked the
crossroads that locals called
Tysons Corner. Today, Tysons
Corner is the commercial
heart of Northern Virginia,
home to the largest single
mall in Greater Washington.
You'll find a Bloomingdale's,
a Nordstrom and 200 other
shops under this roof alone.
✉ 1961 Chain Bridge
Rd, McLean, VA

☎ 703-893-9400
🅜 West Falls Church,
then transfer to Fairfax
Connector 🚌 5B from
L'Enfant Plaza or
Rosslyn Metro stations
🚗 Capital Beltway to
Chain Bridge Rd exit
🕐 Mon-Sat 10am-
9:30pm, Sun 11am-6pm

Tysons Galleria (6, F1)
Also known as Tysons II,
this rival to Tysons Corner
Center (aka Tysons I), just
across the street, features
slightly more upscale
anchor stores (Neiman-
Marcus and Macy's), plus a
hundred or so stores; you
won't need as much stam-
ina to see everything as
you would at Tysons I.
✉ 2001 International
Dr, McLean, VA ☎ 703-
827-7700 🅜 West Falls
Church, then transfer to
Fairfax Connector
🚌 5B from L'Enfant
Plaza or Rosslyn Metro
stations 🚗 Capital
Beltway to Chain
Bridge Rd exit 🕐 Mon-
Sat 10am-9pm, Sun
noon-6pm

The Old Post Office Pavilion harbors a diverse array of shops and stalls.

Rick Gerharter

ANTIQUES & FURNITURE

Choosing between Delft blue and cobalt can be so stressful!

Janis Aldridge (2, D4)
A collection of 17th- to 19th-century prints and engravings is exquisitely framed by an assortment of furniture and other decorative objects from the same period.
✉ 2900 M St NW
☎ 338-7710 Ⓜ Foggy Bottom/GWU 🚌 30, 32, 34, 35, 36, Georgetown shuttles ⏰ Tues-Sat 11am-5 pm

apartment zero
(5, E9) In the ground floor of the building that houses some of the best galleries in the new Penn Quarter, this shop features lamps, tableware and sleek but edgy furniture from new designers like Angela Adams and Karem Rashid and modern masters like Alvar Aalto and Isamu Noguchi.
✉ 406 7th St NW
☎ 628-4067
Ⓜ Archives/Navy Memorial ⏰ Wed-Sat

11am-8pm, Sun noon-5pm

Brass Knob (3, D3)
Almost anything that can be salvaged from an old building finds new life here, from doorknobs to mantelpieces and sinks to stained-glass windows. Quality ranges from near-junk to near-priceless.
✉ 2311 18th St NW
☎ 332-3370 🚌 90,

Old-school storefront

92, 93, 96, 98, L2, U-Link ⏰ Mon-Sat 10:30am-6pm, Sun noon-5pm

Egerton Gardens
(6, J5) Shop for contemporary indoor and outdoor furniture and architectural gee-gaws with an Anglo-Asian look that bring to mind great late-18th-century stylists like Chippendale.
✉ 1117 King St, Alexandria, VA ☎ 703-548-1197 Ⓜ King St ⏰ Mon-Sat 11am-6pm, Sun noon-5pm

Millennium (4, B7)
It might be a new millennium, but the merchandise here harkens back to an old one. Shop for everything your parents threw out in the trash: '50s and '60s furniture, accessories and clothing.
✉ 1528 U St NW
☎ 483-1218

U St/Cardozo
🚌 90, 92, 93, 96, 98,
U-Link ⏰ Thurs-Sun
noon-7pm

Miss Pixie's Furnishings & Whatnot (3, C2)
Poke around a collection of old housewares and furniture that's a step above a junk store. Prepare to be amused.
✉ 1810 Adams Mill Rd
NW ☎ 232-8171
Ⓜ Woodley Park/Zoo
🚌 90, 92, 93, 96, 98,
L2, U-Link ⏰ Thurs
noon-9pm, Fri-Sun
noon-7pm

Random Harvest
(2, C3) Don't believe the name – there's nothing random about this carefully assembled selection of furnishings for home and garden; it's all traditional without being boring or stuffy.
✉ 1313 Wisconsin Ave
NW (also at 810 King St,
Alexandria, VA) ☎ 333-5560 (Alexandria shop
703-548-8820) 🚌 30,
32, 34, 35, 36, George-town shuttles ⏰ Mon-Sat 11am-6pm (Fri to
8pm), Sun noon-6pm

Urban Essentials
(4, B8) Very contemporary furniture and giftware livens up the strip of U St that's putting the 'new' in 'New U.'
✉ 1330 U St NW
☎ 299-0640 Ⓜ U St/
Cardozo 🚌 90, 92, 93,
96, 98, U-Link
⏰ Tues-Fri noon-7pm
(Thurs to 8pm), Sat-Sun
11am-6pm

Vega (5, D9)
Martha Stewart will flush with pride after you lay

down your credit card for a selection of tableware from Vega, a modern home-furnishings store with one of the best collections of design magazines from around the world.
✉ 819 7th St NW
☎ 589-0140 Ⓜ Gallery
Pl/Chinatown ⏰ Tues-Sat 10:30am-6:30pm,
Sun noon-6:30pm

Woven History/Silk Road (4, F11)
Part shop, part museum, this shop fills two rooms with vegetable-dyed, hand-spun wool rugs representing tribes and villages from the Balkans, Central Asia and the Middle East. Come to buy

Old furniture lurks behind old doors in DC.

or just to learn.
✉ 311-315 7th St SE
☎ 543-1705 Ⓜ Eastern
Market ⏰ Tues-Sun
10am-6pm

Georgetown's colonial streets house DC's antique scene.

BOOKS & MUSIC

Chapters (5, C6)
The premier literary book-store in the District features lots of author events and piles of staff selections around the store to guide you through thickets of current offerings.
✉ 1512 K St NW
☎ 347-5495
Ⓜ McPherson Sq
🕑 Mon-Fri 10am-6:30pm, Sat 11am-5pm

DC CD (2, D2)
There's no need to saddle up and head out to a megashop such as Tower Records or HMV when you can instead spend hours and hours pawing through DC CD's selection of almost every kind of music, from opera to rap. There's also a special section devoted to work from local artists.
✉ 2423 18th St NW
☎ 588-1810 Ⓜ Woodley Park/Zoo 🚍 90, 92, 93, 96, L2, U-Link
🕑 Mon-Thurs noon-11pm, Fri noon-1am, Sat 11am-1am, Sun noon-10pm

The city's music scene stems from the days of the Duke.

Flying Saucer Disks (3, D2) A music store with the sensibility of a great old bookstore, Flying Saucer includes a budget CD selection 'in every style, every shape, every color.' A sign says, 'Confused? We spend all our time listening to music, so ask us for suggestions.' They mean it.
✉ 2318 18th St NW
☎ 265-3472 Ⓜ Woodley Park/Zoo 🚍 90, 92, 93, 96, L2, Adams-Morgan shuttle
🕑 Mon-Fri noon-9pm, Sat noon-8pm, Sun noon-6pm

Kramerbooks (4, C6)
There are bigger book-stores in DC, but no better ones. Famous these days for refusing to turn over Monica Lewinsky's reading list to Kenneth Starr's prosecutors, Kramerbooks has been an institution for years because of its amazing assortment of books and magazines, its comfy Afterwords cafe and its late-late hours (24hrs on weekends).
✉ 1517 Connecticut Ave NW ☎ 387-1400
Ⓜ Dupont Circle
🕑 Mon-Thurs 7:30am-1am, Fri 7:30am-Mon 1am

Lambda Rising (4, C6)
Arguably the best gay and lesbian bookstore in the country, it'll keep you posted on the latest

Washington Stories
The best books on Washington are memoirs about its people and their politics. Best of the lot is *Personal History*, the story of Katharine Graham's journey from society child to political wife to the most powerful woman publisher in America. You'll find harsher recollections in her friend Meg Greenfield's *Washington* or Gore Vidal's *Palimpsest*. The capital's political intrigues have also inspired leagues of fiction writers. For an edge-of-your-seat read set in DC, the folks at **Mysterybooks** (1715 Connecticut Ave NW; 4, C6; ☎ 483-1600) recommend Margaret Truman's *Murder in the White House* and Jeffrey Deaver's thriller *The Devil's Teardrop*.

developments in the gay community with a varied selection of books and magazines.
✉ **1625 Connecticut Ave NW** ☎ **462-6969**
Ⓜ **Dupont Circle**
🕐 **Sun-Thurs 10am-10pm, Fri-Sat 10am-midnight**

The Newsroom (4, C6)
In a city that lives on news, there is a surprising dearth of newsstands. The Newsroom, on the north end of the Dupont Circle area, fills the gap with magazines, newspapers, books and tapes in 200 languages (or so they say).
✉ **1803 Connecticut Ave NW** ☎ **462-6657**
Ⓜ **Dupont Circle**
🕐 **7am-9pm**

Olsson's Books & Records (5, E9)
Washington's homegrown chain of independent bookstores has spread to four locations in the city

(Downtown, Georgetown, Dupont Circle and Metro Center) and three more in the 'burbs. The Lansburgh store, with its Footnotes Café, is an anchor of the new Penn Quarter district along 7th St.
✉ **418 7th St NW**
☎ **638-7610**
Ⓜ **Archives/Navy Memorial** 🕐 **Mon-Fri 8am-8pm, Sat 10am-8pm, Sun noon-7:30pm**

Ritmo Latino (3, B3)
The Latin answer to Tower Records, this spanking clean and fresh store looks like it belongs in a mall in Tysons Corner, but for the sound of the music and the foreign-language labels on the racks. Clerks who know their stuff can answer almost any question, in either English or Spanish.
✉ **1775 Columbia Rd NW** ☎ **299-0411**
Ⓜ **Woodley Park/Zoo**
🚌 **42, U-Link** 🕐 **Mon-**

Thurs 9:30am-10pm, Fri-Sat 9:30am-10:15pm, Sun 9:30am-8pm

Second Story Books
(4, C6) Get lost in the stacks of books at the best secondhand bookstore in DC or kill some time among the oddball collections of used posters, LPs and knickknacks.
✉ **2000 P St NW**
☎ **659-8884** Ⓜ **Dupont Circle** 🕐 **10am-7pm**

Travel Books & Language Center
(6, E4) This helpful spot carries travel guides, travel literature, language aids and just about everything else the traveler could ask for, all worth the trek to the Upper Northwest.
✉ **4437 Wisconsin Ave NW** ☎ **237-1322**
Ⓜ **Tenleytown** 🚌 **30, 32, 34, 35, 36,** 🕐 **Mon-Sat 11am-8pm, Sun noon-7pm**

Rick Gerharter

DC's denizens converge on Dupont Circle to satisfy their literary needs.

MARKETS

Adams-Morgan Farmers Market

(3, C2) Every Saturday morning from June to December, farmers from as far afield as Pennsylvania set up their stands in the heart of Adams-Morgan, bringing even more life to the liveliest streets in the District.

✉ **18th & Columbia Rd NW** Ⓜ **Woodley Park/Zoo** 🚌 **42, 90, 92, 93, 96, 98, L2** ⏰ **Jun-Dec Sat 8am-1pm**

DC Farmers Market

(4, C11) This old-fashioned wholesale market, open year-round, sets up shop everyday but Monday between Gallaudet University and the main railroad yards in a distinctly unfashionable stretch of Northeast Washington.

✉ **1309 5th St NE** 🚌 **90, 92, 93** 🚃 **New York Ave east to Florida Ave; right on Florida under the tracks to 5th St** ⏰ **Tues-Thurs 7am-5:30pm, Fri-Sat 7am-6:30pm, Sun 7am-2pm**

Eastern Market

(4, F11) Flea market meets farmers' market meets old-fashioned market hall at Eastern Market, best known as the home of the Market Lunch café. It's good food and drink anytime, and fresh flowers, produce or old furniture on weekends.

✉ **225 7th St SE** ☎ **546-2698** Ⓜ **Eastern Market** ⏰ **indoor stands Tues-Sat 7am-6pm, Sun 8am-4pm; outdoor stands Sat-Sun dawn-late afternoon**

Georgetown Flea Market

(4, C4) Every Sunday morning for the past 29 years, the schoolyard at Georgetown's top end has filled with vendors selling old silver, new sunglasses and everything in between.

✉ **34th St & Wisconsin Ave NW** ☎ **223-0289** 🚌 **30, 32, 34, 35, 36, D1, D2, D3, D6** ⏰ **Sun 9am-5pm**

Takoma Park Farmers' Market

(6, D6) Takoma Park, Greater Washington's answer to Berkeley or Cambridge, was founded by Seventh Day Adventists, who believe in diets heavy on fruits and veggies (among other things). The Sunday farmers' market is one of the best around.

✉ **Laurel Ave btw Eastern & Carroll Aves, Takoma Park, MD** ☎ **301-422-0097** Ⓜ **Takoma** ⏰ **mid-Apr to mid-Dec Sun 10am-2pm**

Eastern Market: How do you like dem apples?

Rick Gerharter

FOOD & DRINK

Bread Line (5, D4)

The best bakery in the city, is equally loved for pizzas, soups and sandwiches available to eat there or to take away. Half the food writers in the District claim owner Mark Furstenberg as a friend; the other half wish they could.

✉ **1751 Pennsylvania Ave NW** ☎ **822-8900** Ⓜ **Farragut West** ⏰ **Mon-Fri 7am-5pm**

Dean & DeLuca

(2, D2) Simply put, this is a terrible place for a diet: every pastry and veggie, artfully arranged and displayed, calls out, 'Take me now.' Don't look at the prices – they'll only disturb you. Just decide what you want, then have it wrapped for a quick getaway or eat it here in the café alongside the market hall.

✉ **3276 M St NW** ☎ **342-2500** Ⓜ **Foggy Bottom/GWU** 🚌 **30, 32, 34, 35, 36, Georgetown shuttles** ⏰ **9am-8pm (Fri-Sat to 9pm)**

Firehook Bakery

(4, C6) Wonderful sour-dough breads made with organic flours compete for attention with enormous cookies and savory sandwiches here in Dupont Circle or at other locations in Downtown, Georgetown and Alexandria.

✉ 1909 Q St NW
☎ 588-9296
Ⓜ Dupont Circle
🕐 Mon-Thurs 7am-8pm, Fri 7am-10pm, Sat 9am-10pm, Sun 9am-8pm

Catch the day's final rays at the Firehook.

Freshfields Whole Foods Market (4, C7)

This big new store has pushed the boundaries of Dupont Circle east, elbowing into an area of storefront churches and bail bondsmen. DC gourmands have already made themselves at home, wandering the grocery and deli.

✉ 1440 P St NW
☎ 332-4300
Ⓜ Dupont Circle
🚌 52, 53, 54, G2
🕐 Mon-Sat 8am-10pm, Sun 8am-9pm

Merkato Market

(3, E2) If you want to learn about Ethiopian cooking, let the people at Merkato educate you on lentils, spices or meats. Not brave enough to make it yourself? Try something from the deli counter or just peruse the bulletin board for news about the East African community.

✉ 2116 18th St NW
☎ 483-9499 🚌 90, 92, 93, 96, 98, L2, U-Link
🕐 Mon-Sat 10am-9pm, Sun 10-6:30pm

Naturally Yours

(5, A3) This hole-in-the-wall stocks organic groceries and food supplements and offers a range of concoctions from the juice bar for people on the go.

✉ 2029 P St NW
☎ 429-1718
Ⓜ Dupont Circle
🕐 Mon-Sat 10am-8pm, Sun 11am-6pm

Safeway (4, C7)

Known locally as the Soviet Safeway because the shelves are so often bare, this Dupont Circle supermarket never lacks for customers, drawing everything from young gay boys to old society matrons.

✉ 1701 Corcoran St NW ☎ 667-6825
Ⓜ Dupont Circle
🕐 6am-11pm

Schneider's of Capitol Hill (5, F15)

One of the best wine shops in DC is shoehorned into 1500 sq ft (150 sq m) and stacked floor to ceiling with wine from everywhere in every price range. The friendly, smart staff are happy to help you or let you wander alone.

✉ 300 Massachusetts Ave NE ☎ 543-9300, 800-377-1461 Ⓜ Union Station 🕐 Mon-Sat 9am-9pm

Viareggio Italian Delicatessen (4, C6)

The smells of an Italian mother's cooking waft out of this old-fashioned deli. Snack on a sub or a slice of pizza or shop for Italian specialties from meats to cheeses to olive oils.

✉ 1727 Connecticut Ave NW ☎ 332-9100
Ⓜ Dupont Circle
🕐 9am-9pm

Coffee Stops

You'll find a **Starbucks** on almost every corner from Capitol Hill to Friendship Heights (sometimes two staring at each other across a street), but there are alternatives. The **Xando** people have brought their formula of daytime coffee, nighttime liquor, to a dozen locations in DC, and the **Caribou Coffee** folks from Chicago are coming to town any day.

CLOTHING & JEWELRY

American in Paris
(6, J5) Or is it a Parisian in America? Joelle Solimano brings to Alexandria casual clothing for women that is very, very carefully designed to prove once again that less is more.
✉ 1225 King St, Alexandria, VA ☎ 703-519-8234 Ⓜ King St ⏰ Mon-Sat 10:30am-7pm, Sun 10:30am-6pm

Betsy Fisher (5, A4)
Working women willing to push the envelope ever so slightly will find suits, dresses and other clothes by Anna Sui and Vivienne Tam, among others.
✉ 1224 Connecticut Ave NW ☎ 785-1975 Ⓜ Dupont Circle ⏰ Mon-Fri 10am-7pm (Thurs to 8pm), Sat 10am-6pm

Britches of Georgetown (2, C3)
One of the great founts of American preppy style is getting a little tired (like American preppy style itself), but if you're in the market for a blazer or something in madras, it's a great alternative to Brooks Brothers or Polo.
✉ 1247 Wisconsin Ave NW ☎ 338-3330

Fortunately, DC's fashion scene has progressed recently.

🚌 30, 32, 34, 35, 36, G2, Georgetown shuttles ⏰ Mon-Sat 10am-7pm (Thurs to 9pm), Sun noon-6pm

Daisy (3, C2)
Andrea Paro and Fabiana Mesquita have lined the racks of their boutique with low-rise slacks and other contemporary girly-girl clothes perfect for clubbing.
✉ 1814 Adams Mill Rd NW ☎ 797-1777 Ⓜ Woodley Park/Zoo 🚌 90, 92, 93, 96, L2, Adams-Morgan shuttle ⏰ Mon & Wed-Sat noon-8pm, Sun 2-6pm

Imagine (6, J5)
Rich, unusual fabrics come in unusual shapes at this shop, which features unique women's clothing and jewelry with an arts and crafts flair (eg, a silk opera jacket printed with a Japanese-woodblock-like design).
✉ 1124 King St, Alexandria, VA ☎ 703-548-1461 Ⓜ King St ⏰ Mon-Sat 10am-7pm, Sun 11am-5pm

Meep's (4, B7)
To escape the buttoned-down masses, head to this funky spot, which features two floors filled with vintage clothing for men and women and accessories to match.
✉ 1520 U St NW ☎ 265-6546 Ⓜ U St/Cardozo 🚌 90, 92, 93, 94, 96, 98 U-Link ⏰ Mon-Thurs 4-7pm, Fri 4-8pm, Sat noon-8pm, Sun noon-6pm

Niagara (3, D2)
A welcome exception to the general rule that

Second Time Around
You won't find a lot of stores selling used clothes, but you will find a couple of great consignment stores where penny-wise Washington men and women put last year's models on the racks for your consideration. Two of the best are **Designer Too Consignments** (3404 Connecticut Ave NW; 6, E5; ☎ 686-6303), in Cleveland Park, and **Secondi** (1702 Connecticut Ave NW; 4, C6; ☎ 667-1122), near Dupont Circle.

there's nothing special on the shelves in the capital, Niagara sells some of the highest-style casual clothing in DC: clean, crisp, almost architectural clothes for both women and men.

✉ 2423 18th St NW
☎ 332-7474 Ⓜ Woodley Park/Zoo 🚌 90, 92, 93, 96, L2, Adams-Morgan shuttle
🕐 Mon 3-8pm, Wed noon-8pm, Fri-Sat noon-9pm, Sun 1-6pm

Saks-Jandel (6, D4) Looking for a little something to wear to the opera or one of those benefits listed in *Washingtonian* magazine? Try this

collection of very-high-fashion boutiques: Fendi, St Laurent, Celine and Christian Dior.

✉ 5510 Wisconsin Ave NW, Chevy Chase, MD
☎ 301-652-2250
Ⓜ Friendship Hts
🕐 Mon-Sat 10am-6pm

Shake Your Booty (3, D2) Part of the group of boutiques that's endeavoring to make Adams-Morgan safe for fashionistas, this shop specializes in high-style shoes and accessories for young women who can't get enough of them.

✉ 2324 18th St NW
☎ 518-8205
Ⓜ Woodley Park/Zoo

🚌 90, 92, 93, 96, L2, Adams-Morgan Shuttle
🕐 Mon & Wed-Sat noon-9pm, Sun noon-6pm

Up Against the Wall (2, D2) Listen to all the current music from the DJ while shopping for the latest T from Mossimo or picking through the inventory of hip streetwear and club clothes.

✉ 3219 M St NW
☎ 337-9316 Ⓜ Foggy Bottom/GWU 🚌 30, 32, 34, 35, 36, Georgetown shuttles
🕐 Mon-Thurs 10am-9pm, Fri-Sat 10am-10pm, Sun 11am-7pm

ARTS & CRAFTS

Appalachian Spring (5, E14) A huge array of arts and crafts pieces from all over America almost fills the East Vestibule of Union Station.

✉ Union Station, 50 Massachusetts Ave NE (also at 1415 Wisconsin Ave NW in

Georgetown) ☎ 682-0505 Ⓜ Union Station
🕐 Mon-Sat 10am-9pm, Sun noon-6pm

Artcraft Collection (6, J5) Scores of US artisans have crafted the furniture, ceramics, jewelry,

glassware, wood pieces and other cool stuff here – all concrete proof that you can do serious work and still have fun.

✉ 132 King St, Alexandria, VA ☎ 703-299-6616 Ⓜ King St
🕐 Mon-Sat 11am-9pm, Sun 11am-8pm

Rick Gerharter

Union Station's Grand Concourse, home to the kitsch and the classy

Beadazzled (4, C6)
Browse through case after case of beads, plus all the stuff you'll need to string them and books to tell you how to do it, or opt for the ethnic jewelry and textiles that are ready to wear.
✉ **1507 Connecticut Ave NW ☎ 265-2323** Ⓜ **Dupont Circle** ◷ **Mon-Sat 10am-8pm, Sun 11am-6pm**

Elder Crafters of Alexandria (6, J5)
This nonprofit cooperative features work by crafts-people over age 55. Step inside to see the Amish quilts and linger over the pottery and the children's clothes.
✉ **405 Cameron St, Alexandria, VA ☎ 703-683-4338** Ⓜ **King St** ◷ **Tue-Sat 10am-5pm, Sun noon-5pm**

Ginza (4, C6)
Spend a little or spend a lot at this tiny storefront crammed with Japanese arts and crafts, from chopstick rests to textiles and tansu chests.
✉ **1721 Connecticut Ave NW ☎ 331-7991** Ⓜ **Dupont Circle** ◷ **Mon-Sat 11am-7pm, Sun noon-5pm**

Indian Craft Shop (5, F4) The Department of the Interior runs the Bureau of Indian Affairs, so it's not surprising to find a gift shop tucked inside DOI headquarters, just off the Mall. What may be surpris-ing, however, is the quality of some of the textiles, carvings and pottery on hand.
✉ **1849 C St NW, Room 1023 ☎ 208-4056** Ⓜ **Foggy Bottom/GWU** ◷ **Mon-Fri 8:30am-4:30pm**

Ten Thousand Villages (6, J5)
A chain store with a differ-ence, this belongs to a group of 40 nonprofit shops run by a Mennonite affiliate, selling handicrafts to promote fair trade and preserve cultural traditions. The goods match the beauty of the ideals.
✉ **824 King St, Alexandria, VA ☎ 703-684-1435** Ⓜ **King St** ◷ **Tues-Sat 11am-7pm, Sun noon-5pm**

The Village (4, F11)
Find clothing, jewelry and craftwork on the ground floor and artwork on the 2nd floor of this charming Capitol Hill gallery.
✉ **705 North Carolina Ave SE ☎ 546-3040** Ⓜ **Eastern Market** ◷ **Tues-Fri 11am-6pm, Sat 10am-6pm, Sun noon-4pm**

Yawa Books & Gifts (3, E3) Baskets, boxes and other handiwork from the West Indies and Africa complement a broad selec-tion of books by and for African Americans.
✉ **2206 18th St NW ☎ 483-6805** 🚌 **90, 92, 93, 96, 98, L2, U-Link** ◷ **Mon, Wed & Fri 11am-8pm; Tues & Thurs 11am-7pm; Sat 11am-9pm**

Rick Gerharter

Old Town Alexandria boasts a full complement of arts and crafts shops.

FOR CHILDREN

DC: a great place for a romp

FAO Schwarz (2, D2)
You can run but you can't hide from the most opulent toy emporium in America. On the other hand, if you can stand the noise, you can occupy kids for hours here, letting them roam around through the aisles to their hearts' content.
✉ **Georgetown Park Mall, 3222 M St NW** ☎ **965-7000** Ⓜ **Foggy Bottom/GWU** 🚌 **30, 32, 34, 35, 36, Georgetown shuttles** ⏰ Mon-Sat 10am-9pm, Sun noon-6pm

Flights of Fancy
(5, E14) Thomas the Train and Biro sets are only some of the attractions at this refined toy shop, which specializes in things with wheels.
✉ **Union Station, 50 E Massachusetts Ave NE** ☎ **371-9800** Ⓜ **Union Station** ⏰ Mon-Sat 10am-9pm, Sun noon-6pm

Left Bank (4, C6)
You don't have to be a kid to shop here, just a person of taste (or French taste) who appreciates such icons of style as Babar, Madeleine and Tintin. You can also shop for wonderful gift stuff for people of all ages, not all of it French but almost all of it sharp.
✉ **1627 Connecticut Ave NW** ☎ **518-4000** Ⓜ **Dupont Circle** ⏰ Sun-Wed 10am-7pm, Thurs-Sat 10am-8pm

A Likely Story (6, J5)
This cozy bookstore for children features year-round story hours four times a week for kids of all ages.
✉ **1555 King St, Alexandria, VA** ☎ **703-836-2498** Ⓜ **King St** ⏰ Mon-Sat 10am-6pm, Sun 1-5pm

Madeleine's Kids
(6, J5) At this consignment shop for kids' wear, pick up the kind of fancy clothes that grandmothers with bucks buy new and pay only a fraction of the original cost.
✉ **1521 King St, Alexandria, VA** ☎ **703-836-9046** Ⓜ **King St** ⏰ Mon-Sat 11am-5pm

National Gallery of Art (5, G10)
There's a special store for children inside the big gallery shop under the West Wing of the NGA. Check out the games and puzzles, the art books and storybooks, and lots of different activity kits.
✉ **6th St & Constitution Ave NW** ☎ **737-4215** Ⓜ **Archives/Navy Memorial** ⏰ Mon-Sat 10am-5pm, Sun 11am-6pm

Sullivan's Toy Store
(6, E4) If you can't bear Toys 'R' Us or FAO, come to this neighborhood institution that's been specializing in European and educational toys for over 40 years.
✉ **3412 Wisconsin Ave NW** ☎ **363-1343** 🚌 **30, 32, 34, 35, 36** ⏰ Mon, Tues & Sat 10am-6pm, Wed-Fri 10am-7pm, Sun noon-5pm

Why Not? (6, J5)
The merchandise at this little department store for kids in the middle of Old Town, Alexandria, ranges from practical clothes that moms buy to fancy stuff that grandmoms buy, along with toys and books and odds and ends.
✉ **200 King St, Alexandria, VA** ☎ **703-548-4420** Ⓜ **King St** ⏰ Mon 10am-5:30pm, Tues-Sat 10am-9pm, Sun noon-5pm

Watch out for the shadow!

SPECIALTY SHOPS

Georgetown Tobacco
(2, D3) Tobacco gave birth to Georgetown, so it's fitting that there's a good, traditional tobacco shop right on Georgetown's main drag. For some reason, the store also carries the largest selection of Panama hats this side of Florida.
✉ 3144 M St NW
☎ 338-5160 Ⓜ Foggy Bottom/GWU 🚌 30, 32, 34, 35, 36, Georgetown shuttles ⏱ Mon-Sat 10am-9pm, Sun noon-8pm

Havana Max (2, D2)
If you're looking for a hookah, neon glow glasses or temporary tattoos, come to Havana Max: part head shop, part gadget shop, part warehouse for the club set where you can rent strobes and lights for your next party.
✉ 3249 M St NW
☎ 337-8897 Ⓜ Foggy Bottom/GWU 🚌 30, 32, 34, 35, 36, Georgetown shuttles ⏱ Mon-Thurs noon-10pm, Fri-Sat noon-2am, Sun noon-9pm

Home Rule (4, C7)
Fun, stylish homewares for the kitchen, the bath or the office include wastebaskets

by Karem Rashid (designer of the moment) and wire-mesh file systems by Design Ideas. It's good taste at great prices.
✉ 1807 14th St NW
☎ 797-5544 Ⓜ U St/Cardozo ⏱ Tues-Sat 11am-7pm, Sun noon-5pm

House of Musical Traditions (6, D6)
Takoma Park is 20min by Metro from Downtown DC, but it's closer to Berkeley or Amsterdam in spirit. HOMT is a case in point: it sells drums, guitars, banjos, and CDs of folk and jazz by artists from the neighborhood and far, far away.
✉ 7040 Carroll Ave, Takoma Park, MD
☎ 301-270-9090
Ⓜ Takoma 🚌 S2
⏱ Sun-Mon 11am-5pm, Tues-Sat 11am-7pm

Pet Essentials (4, C7)
Buy all-natural pet foods or holistic supplements, or pick up a knickknack to take home for your pet at this combination pet store and gift shop. If you're traveling with Rover, check out the pet daycare next door.
✉ 1722 14th St NW
☎ 986-7907
Ⓜ U St/Cardozo

🚌 52, 53, 54
⏱ Mon-Sat 10am-8pm, Sun 11am-5pm

simply home (4, C6)
This shop may be described as 'Martha Stewart goes to Thailand,' or better put, 'Martha Stewart comes home from Thailand.' Proprietors Nannapat Pollert, Sak Pollert and Alan Parnploy have collected enough exotic furnishings and accessories to fill up a beautiful store.
✉ 1811B 18th St NW
☎ 986-8607 Ⓜ Dupont Circle 🚌 L2 ⏱ Tues-Fri noon-10pm, Sat 11am-10pm, Sun 11am-9pm

Ultra Violet (2, D3)
A flower shop masquerading as a gallery, Ultra Violet features long-stemmed beauties flown in from as far a field as California or the Netherlands. The banker's hours kept at the shop reflect the fact that the shop owners spend weekends beautifying big events around town.
✉ 1061 31st St NW
☎ 333-3002 Ⓜ Foggy Bottom/GWU 🚌 30, 32, 34, 35, 36, Georgetown Shuttles ⏱ Mon-Fri 9am-5pm, weekends by appointment

Souvenir Stands

Souvenir stands line the Mall, all offering the same assortment of baseball caps, postcards and T-shirts (FBI shirts and stars-and-stripes varieties are perennial favorites). This is where you go for a snow globe that contains a little White House or Washington Monument. If you're looking for a more stylish keepsake, head to the museum shops at the **Smithsonian** (p. 24) or the arcades at **Union Station** (p. 37).

Rick Gerharter

places to eat

Before Camelot (ie, the Kennedy Administration), 'Washington Food' meant navy bean soup at the Senate Dining Room. Jackie Kennedy brought Rene Verdon and serious cooking to the White House, as she brought Pablo Casals and serious culture to the East Room. Verdon left the White House after the Johnsons arrived but not before Washington developed a taste for classic French cooking that survives to the present.

Today, Washington food runs the gamut from empanada stands to chichi dining rooms serving classic Italian or modern American. There's still next to no Chinese food and not much Japanese or Korean, but DC boasts a range of Middle Eastern restaurants equal to any city in the country, some good Vietnamese and Thai, and the best assortment of African restaurants this side of the Atlantic.

Whatever you want, you can enjoy it outdoors six months a year. The evenings are mild and the sidewalks are wide, so Washingtonians have taken to café living as if they were Parisians. On a warm summer night, with a great meal before you and a great street scene behind you, you can take to it yourself.

How Much?
The symbols used in this chapter indicate the cost of a main course, without drinks, tax or tips.

$	under $12
$$	$12-17
$$$	$18-24
$$$$	over $24

Rick Gerharter

Drinks
Most restaurants serve alcohol (beware, though: the drinking age throughout the USA is 21, and lots of places ask for ID) and most restaurants offer house wines or a selection of wines by the glass (the latter are usually superior to house wines). You'll find a decent selection of beers in most places, a great selection in a few.

Tipping
As elsewhere in the US, tipping is customary in restaurants. Servers expect 15-20% of the check total before tax. Give a little more if the service was exceptional and a little less if it wasn't. Many restaurants add a service charge for parties of six or more. If you're traveling with a gang, check the check before you tip. Tipping is optional at coffee bars and places where you place your own order at the counter. Fifty cents or a dollar is in order if you ask for something complicated like a double half-caff latte with non-fat soy milk.

Opening Hours
Most restaurants, cafés and the like are open seven days a week, but there are those that close on Sunday or Monday night. Specific opening hours for each establishment listed are included in the reviews throughout this chapter.

Meal Times

Federal employees work flex-times, so some people start work very early and others start very late. Congress works through the afternoon and evening, which further complicates scheduling. People eat breakfast at any time between 6 and 9am, either at home or near work. Lunch, usually eaten close to work, starts at noon or 1pm; dinnertime begins about 7pm. A surprisingly good number of places stay open very late, even on weekdays, despite the city's somewhat deserved reputation as a sleepy Southern town.

After Hours

If you're looking for sustenance after the bars close, **The Diner** (p. 73) serves meals around the clock Kramerbooks and its attached café, **Afterwords** (p. 81), stay open from Friday morning until 1am Monday. For something more substantial, try the **Bistro Français** (p. 83), which closes at 3am Sunday to Thursday, 4am Friday and Saturday.

Booking Tables

Most but not all moderate to high-priced restaurants ($$ and up) take reservations for lunch and dinner, so call ahead. Outside seating is almost always first-come, first-served, even with a reservation. Many restaurants that take reservations also set seats aside for walk-ins, so don't hesitate to ask. Restaurants that don't take reservations frequently subject customers to long waits (20 minutes or more), so ease into it or find another place.

Prolonged studying without proper nutrition can lead to headaches. Eat something!

Rick Gerharter

ADAMS-MORGAN

The strip of 18th St from Kalorama to Columbia Rds is the liveliest place to eat and drink in town – so lively that the police often close part of the street on the weekends to accommodate the crowds.

Arbor (3, D2) $$
Modern American
The menu is a bit of a mishmash – a page of salads and sandwiches, a page of entrees, a page of light dishes – but everything that emerges on the plates is as elegant as the space on the 18th St sidewalk. It's a particularly sweet place to eat outside on a summer evening and take in the parade.
✉ 2400 18th St NW
☎ 667-1200 Ⓜ Dupont Circle ⊟ L2 ⊘ Sun & Tue-Thurs 5:30-10pm, Fri-Sat 5:30-11pm, brunch Sat-Sun 11am-3pm Ⓥ

Bukom Café (3, C2) $
African
The cuisine hails from West, not East, Africa, so don't expect Ethiopian specialties. Instead, try crushed melon seeds with spinach, deep-fried snapper with onions, tomatoes, peppers and ginger or other dishes from Ghana and the Côte d'Ivoire.
✉ 2442 18th St NW
☎ 265-4600 Ⓜ Woodley Park/Zoo ⊟ 42, 90, 92, 93, 94, 96, 98 U-Link ⊘ 4pm-2am (Fri-Sat to 3am) ⅙ Ⓥ

Cashion's Eat Place (3, C2) $$$
Modern American
The kind of spot that gives American cooking a good name, Cashion's serves food that can be light and rich at the same time (or just rich and rich, as in duck breast served with

Rick Gerharter

Using the Force to select fruit

foie gras). It's not cheap, but it's worth every buck.
✉ 1819 Columbia Rd NW ☎ 797-1819 Ⓜ Woodley Park/Zoo ⊟ 42, Adams-Morgan shuttle ⊘ Sun & Tues 5:30-10pm, Wed-Sat 5:30-11pm, brunch Sun 11:30am-2:30pm Ⓥ

Cities (3, D2) $$$
Modern American
The Cities people used to travel the world to bring back a different menu every year – Naples one year, Istanbul the next. They've stopped indefinitely in Barcelona, and their homage to Catalunya is sensational.
✉ 2424 18th St NW
☎ 328-2100 Ⓜ Woodley Park/Zoo, Dupont Circle ⊟ L2, Adams-Morgan shuttle ⊘ Sun-Thurs 6-11pm, Fri-Sat 6pm-12:30am Ⓥ

The Diner (3, C2) $
American
What you see is what you get – straightforward

American café food, reasonably done, served in a nice room with a friendly crowd around. It's 'round-the-clock service, to boot.
✉ 2453 18th St NW
☎ 232-8800 Ⓜ Woodley Park/Zoo ⊟ 42, 90, 92, 93, 94, 96, 98 U-Link ⊘ 24hrs ⅙ Ⓥ

Grill From Ipanema (3, C2) $$$
Brazilian
This Southern Brazilian–style grill serves gaucho fare like steaks and sausages and spicy African-influenced dishes from the north, including *feijoida* (Brazil's answer to cassoulet) or *bobo de camarao* (shrimp stew). The stylish bar adds *caipirinhas* and samba sounds to the mix.
✉ 1858 Columbia Rd NW ☎ 986-0757 Ⓜ Woodley Park/Zoo ⊟ 42, 90, 92, 93, 94, 96, 98 U-Link ⊘ Mon-Thurs 5-10:30pm, Fri 5pm-midnight, Sat noon-midnight, Sat noon-10pm

I Matti (3, D2) $$
Italian

A plain-spoken trattoria amid the hubbub of Adams-Morgan, this is one of the better places around for a simple Italian meal, though locals take points off for inconsistency.

✉ 2436 18th St NW
☎ 462-8844 Ⓜ Woodley Park/Zoo 🚌 42, 90, 92, 93, 94, 96, 98 U-Link ☉ Sun-Thurs 5:30-10pm, Fri-Sat 5:30-11pm ♿ Ⓥ

La Fourchette (3, C2) $$
French

Family-run La Fourchette has been turning out good bistro food at good bistro prices year after year. Come enjoy old standbys like escargots or bouillabaisse and remember why you fell in love with them years ago.

✉ 2429 18th St NW
☎ 332-3077
Ⓜ Woodley Park/Zoo 🚌 42, 90, 92, 93, 94, 96, 98 U-Link ☉ Mon-Thurs 11:30am-10:30pm, Fri 11:30am-11pm, Sat 4-11pm, Sun 4-9:30pm ♿

Mama Ayesha's (3, B1) $
Middle Eastern

Want to know what meals cost in the 1950s? Come to this neighborhood institution, where the prices and the decor have changed little in 50 years. Mama's specializes in Syrian takes on hummus, kebabs and other Levantine classics.

✉ 1967 Calvert St NW
☎ 232-5431
Ⓜ Woodley Park/Zoo 🚌 90, 92, 93, 94, 96, 98 U-Link ☉ 11am-midnight ♿ Ⓥ

Meskerem Ethiopian Restaurant (3, D2) $
East African

If you've wanted to try Ethiopian cooking but you're not sure where to begin, this is the place to get the lowdown on how to scoop up your *wat* (savory stews, meat or vegetarian) with your *injera* (spongy Ethiopian bread).

✉ 2434 18th St NW
☎ 462-1100
Ⓜ Woodley Park/Zoo 🚌 42, 90, 92, 93, 94, 96, 98 U-Link ☉ noon-midnight (Fri-Sat to 1am) ♿ Ⓥ

Pasta Mia (3, C2) $$
Italian

People line up on the sidewalk for generous servings of 20-some kinds of pasta made the way your mother would do it if your mother were (a) Italian and (b) a great cook with a light hand.

✉ 1790 Columbia Rd
☎ 328-9114 Ⓜ Woodley Park/Zoo 🚌 42, 90, 92, 93, 94, 96, 98 U-Link ☉ Mon-Sat 6:30-10:30pm Ⓥ

Perry's (3, C2) $$$
Japanese

Perry's is an unlikely combination – campy and Japanese. Some come to try some of the best sushi in Washington but even more head here for the view of Adams-Morgan from the rooftop deck and for the drag brunch on Sunday.

✉ 1811 Columbia Rd
☎ 234-6218
Ⓜ Woodley Park/Zoo 🚌 42, 90, 92, 93, 94, 96, 98 U-Link ☉ Sun-Thurs 5:30-11:30pm, Fri-Sat 5:30pm-12:30am, brunch Sunday 11:30am-3pm

Red Sea (3, C2) $
Ethiopian

A perennial favorite on all the local lists of ethnic and bargain restaurants, Red Sea offers a feast of traditional meat and vegetable stews on injera bread, plus a range of appetizers and side dishes. Try a couple of medium orders of the main courses or the sides to make up your own tasting menu.

✉ 2463 18th St NW
☎ 483-5000 Ⓜ Woodley Park/Zoo 🚌 42, 90, 92, 93, 94, 96, 98 U-Link ☉ 11am-10:30pm ♿ Ⓥ

Room with a View

There are no towers inside the District, and not a lot of hills, so you won't have many opportunities for enjoying a vista with your food. Your best bets for river views are **Sequoia** (p. 84), the **Roof Terrace Restaurant** (☎ 416-8555) at the **Kennedy Center** (p. 17) or **Phillips Flagship** (p. 85), which overlooks the Washington Channel. The roof deck at **Perry's** (p. 74) offers a sensational view of Adams-Morgan. The café on the **Hotel Washington**'s roof (p. 101) features a city vista. Finally, if you dine in **Pavilion Café** at the National Gallery of Art (p. 21), you can contemplate sculpture by artists like Claes Oldenberg.

ALEXANDRIA (OLD TOWN)

La Madeleine (6, J5) **$**
French
A French cafeteria? Parisian cuisine unexpectedly hits the fast track at La Madeleine, as diners line up for flaky pastries as well as French-accented American dishes such as salads and sandwiches. The dinner menu should please dedicated Francophiles more than the lunch offerings, but you'll find a good meal at a good price either time.
✉ 500 King St, Alexandria, VA (also at 3000 M St NW in Georgetown) ☎ 703-739-2584 Ⓜ King St ① Sun-Thurs 7am-10pm, Fri-Sat 7am-11pm ♿ Ⓥ

Lite Fair (6, J5) **$**
American
This old-fashioned, nothing-special coffee shop attempts to get a little creative with the chicken tempura and the sole almondine, but you're probably better off sticking with the basics: burgers or club sandwiches.
✉ 1018 King St, Alexandria, VA ☎ 703-549-3717 Ⓜ King St ① Mon 11am-3pm, Tues-Thurs 11am-9pm, Fri-Sat 11am-10pm ♿

Majestic Cafe (6, J5) **$$**
Modern American
Modern American cooking speaks with a Southern accent here. To start, try the sautéed chicken breast with country ham and add a side of hush puppies, but leave room for plum dumpling or layer cake. Children's portions are available.
✉ 911 King St, Alexandria, VA ☎ 703-837-9117 Ⓜ King St ① lunch Tues-Sat 11:30am-2:30pm; dinner Sun & Tues-Thurs 5:30-10pm, Fri-Sat 5:30-11pm ♿ Ⓥ

ARLINGTON

Hard Times Cafe (4, F1) **$**
American
Four kinds of chili – Texas (hot), Cincinnati (sweet, with cinnamon), Terlingua (from the famous chili cook-offs in Terlingua, Texas) and vegetarian (say no more) – come with classic American honky-tonk food like chicken wings.
✉ 3028 Wilson Blvd, Arlington, VA ☎ 703-528-2233 Ⓜ Clarendon ① Mon-Thurs 11:30am-10pm, Fri-Sat 11:30am-11pm, Sun noon-10pm ♿ Ⓥ

Queen Bee (4, F1) **$**
Vietnamese
Widely regarded as the best Vietnamese restaurant in Greater Washington, Queen Bee offers bowls of steaming *pho* (Hanoi-style beef soup), savory grilled entrees like Vietnamese steak or Hanoi grilled pork, and such sweet delights as shrimp on sugarcane.
✉ 3181 Wilson Blvd, Arlington, VA ☎ 703-527-3444 Ⓜ Clarendon ① 11am-10pm ♿ Ⓥ

Red, Hot & Blue (4, F1) **$**
Barbecue
Come here for Memphis-style barbecue – pork ribs served wet or dry, pulled pork or pork sausages and sides of beans, slaw and potato salad. Those who prefer to eschew the pig can opt instead for chicken, brisket or turkey links.
✉ 3014 Wilson Blvd, Arlington, VA ☎ 703-243-1510 Ⓜ Clarendon ① Sun-Thurs 11am-10pm, Fri-Sat 11am-11pm ♿

The river provides good eatin' in Northern Virginia.

CAPITOL HILL

Government regulations forbid lobbyists from giving gifts – including free meals – worth more than $10, so you'll find lots of spots around Capitol Hill with lunch specials for $9.95.

Berlin (5, F15)   **$$**
German
Deutsch dishes like sauerbraten, *jagerschnitzel* (pork cutlet) and a *wurstplatte* (sausage platter) share the stage with Continental cuisine (eg, pork tenderloin with a mushroom duxelle). Lunch fare is generally lighter – try the wurst salad, which brings to mind Helmut Kohl on a diet.
✉ **322 Massachusetts Ave NE** ☎ **544-7425**
Ⓜ **Union Station** ◷ **Mon-Thurs 11:30am-10pm, Fri-Sat 11:30am-11pm, Sun 4-10pm** **V**

Centre Café (5, E14) **$**
American
Watch the world hustle by from center of the main concourse of Union Station. The all-American bar-and-grill fare includes Caesar salads and Santa Fe–style red-chili chicken, plus some local specialities like Maryland crab cakes.
✉ **Union Station, 50 Massachusetts Ave NE** ☎ **682-0143** Ⓜ **Union Station** ◷ **Mon-Fri**

8am-10pm, Sat-Sun 11:30am-10pm

The Dubliner (5, E13)   **$$**
Irish
The phrase 'Irish cuisine' is no longer an oxymoron. The traditional dishes here (corned beef and cabbage, London broil, and shepherd's pie) promise to delight your mouth and nose. Stay after 9pm, when the place turns into one of the best Irish bars in town, and enjoy performances that please the eye and ear.
✉ **520 N Capitol St** ☎ **737-3773** Ⓜ **Union Station** ◷ **breakfast Mon-Sat 7-10am; lunch & dinner Mon-Sat 11am-1am, Sun 11am-midnight** ⚹

East St Cafe (5, E14) **$**
Pan-Asian
The menu of tasty noodles and stir-fries from East Asia and Southeast Asia includes Filipino dishes that usually don't make the pan-Asian or fusion menus. This place offers something for everyone, whether you

need it hot, crave it sweet, wish it with veggies or want it with meat.
✉ **Union Station, 50 Massachusetts Ave NE** ☎ **371-6788** Ⓜ **Union Station** ◷ **Mon-Fri 11am-9pm, Fri-Sat 1-8pm** ⚹ **V**

Il Radicchio (5, H15)   **$**
Italian
Choose your pasta from column A on the menu, choose your sauce from column B, then chow down – it couldn't be simpler at this inexpensive spot run by the proprietor of Galileo, one of the priciest Italian restaurants in town. Those tired of pasta can pick pizza or panini.
✉ **223 Pennsylvania Ave SE** ☎ **547-5114** Ⓜ **Eastern Market** ◷ **Mon-Thurs 11:30am-10pm, Fri-Sat 11:30am-11pm, Sun 5-9pm** ⚹ **V**

La Loma (5, F15)   **$**
Mexican
Stick to the classics on the menu – the tacos, burritos, enchiladas and chimichangas (deep-fried burritos) –

Big Deals

As mentioned above, it's not a good idea to try to bribe congresspeople with tony lunches (soft money is the way to go). However, if you're not entertaining a member of the legislature and you have fish to fry, spend a few more bucks to make a deal at **The Palm** (1225 19th St NW; 5, B4; ☎ 293-9091), **La Colline** (400 N Capitol St; 5, E13; ☎ 737-0400), **Vidalia** (p. 80) or **Legal Sea Foods** (p. 80). None of them is easy on the wallet, but all will thrill the palate.

Rick Gerharter

and you'll come away happy and full. In a city not known for Mexican food, this is one of the few places to get a good south-of-the-border meal.
✉ 316 Massachusetts Ave NE ☎ 548-2550 Ⓜ Union Station ⏲ lunch 11:30am-2:30pm, dinner Sun-Thurs 5:30-10:30pm, Fri-Sat 5:30-11pm ♿ V

Le Bon Café
(5, H14) $
French-American
American breakfast pastries, salads and sandwiches get a French touch at this café, a sensational alternative to the cafeterias on Capitol Hill. The food is light and delectable – from a tuna niçoise to a croque monsieur to a grilled Portobello sandwich with pesto and slow-roasted tomatoes on a baguette.
✉ 210 2nd St SE ☎ 547-7200 Ⓜ Capitol South ⏲ Mon-Fri 7:30am-5pm, Sat-Sun 8:30am-3:30pm ♿ V

Market Lunch
(4, F11) $
Southern
The place for breakfast or lunch on the Hill, Market Lunch will fill you up with big Southern-style plates of ham and eggs or pancakes in the morning or lunchtime seasonal specialties like soft-shell crab sandwiches or fried perch.
✉ Eastern Market, 225 7th St SE ☎ 547-8444 Ⓜ Eastern Market ⏲ Tues-Sat 7:30am-3pm, Sun 11am-3pm ♿

B Smith (5, E14) $$
Southern
High-stepping Southern cooking in a high-style

If dining alone, bring a book or spy on conversations.

dining room will put meat on your bones and a smile on your face. The menu hails from Louisiana (red beans and rice, jambalaya) and South Carolina (seafood Charleston, served over Reggiano-cheddar grits).
✉ Union Station, 50 Massachusetts Ave NE ☎ 289-6188 Ⓜ Union Station ⏲ lunch Mon-Sat 11:30am-4pm, Sun 11:30am-3pm; dinner Mon-Thurs 5-10pm, Fri-Sat 5-11pm, Sun 5-9pm ♿

Thai Roma (5, H15) $
Fusion
They eat noodles in Italy and in Bangkok. And if you walk down the sidewalk on Capitol Hill you'll see happy people eating Italian pasta with Thai spices, or Thai soups and salads.
✉ 313 Pennsylvania Ave SE ☎ Eastern Market ⏲ 11:30am-10:30pm (Fri-Sat to 11:30pm) ♿ V

Tortilla Coast
(5, J14) $
Tex-Mex
This Capitol Hill drinking spot dishes up decent Tex-Mex fare in a fun, noisy space. Note the Barry

White quote on the menu: 'It's cool to share.'
✉ 400 1st St SE ☎ 546-6768 Ⓜ Capitol South ⏲ Mon-Wed 11:30am-10pm, Thurs-Fri 11:30am-11pm, Sat noon-10pm ♿

Two Quail (5, F15) $$
Continental
Enjoy French-inflected food, such as seared duck breasts or quail stuffed with raspberries, in a room that makes all the DC romantic-dining shortlists.
✉ 320 Massachusetts Ave NE ☎ 543-8030 Ⓜ Union Station ⏲ lunch Mon-Fri 11:30am-2:30pm, dinner Sun-Thurs 5-10pm, Fri-Sat 5-11pm V

Tune Inn of Capitol Hill (5, H15) $
American
The kind of dive where you decide what you're going to drink first, Tune Inn does boast the best burger on the Hill and serves bar snacks like mini crab cakes (a distinctly local touch).
✉ 331½ Pennsylvania Ave SE ☎ 543-2725 Ⓜ Eastern Market ⏲ Sun-Thurs 8am-2am, Fri-Sat 8am-3am

CLEVELAND PARK

Cleveland Park has two commercial strips: along Connecticut Ave near the Cleveland Park Metro station and along Wisconsin Ave north of Washington National Cathedral, which is accessible by car or by bus from Georgetown.

Ardeo (6, E5) $$
Modern American
The dining room at Ardeo is almost too hip for comfort, but the menu will put you at ease with standards ranging from burgers to roast chicken to soft-shell crabs, all served with wonderful sides like mashed potatoes and steamed veggies.
✉ 3311 Connecticut Ave NW ☎ 244-6750
Ⓜ Cleveland Park
🚌 L1, L2, L4 ⏰ Mon-Thurs 5:30-10:30pm, Fri-Sat 5:30-11:30pm, Sun 11am-10:30pm ♿ Ⓥ

Cafe Deluxe
(6, E4) $$
American
American bar-and-grill food is nicely done and nicely served in a room that recalls Galatoire's in New Orleans. The steak frites would pass muster in a bistro; the chicken pot pie would pass muster at your mother's.
✉ 3228 Wisconsin Ave NW ☎ 686-2233
🚌 30, 32, 34, 35, 36
⏰ Mon-Thurs 11:30am-10:30pm, Fri-Sat 11:30am-11pm, Sun 11am-11pm ♿ Ⓥ

Abundant fruit keeps Washingtonians healthy.

Rick Gerharter

Coppi's Vigorelli
(6, E5) $$
Italian
The people who brought pizza and yuppies to U St have brought a Ligurian trattoria to Cleveland Park. Lots of dishes get their flavor from a wood-fired oven, including a daily oven-baked rice dish and other *cucina povera* (peasant food) from the north.
✉ 3421 Connecticut Ave NW ☎ 244-6437
Ⓜ Cleveland Park
🚌 L1, L2, L4 ⏰ Sun-Thurs 5-11pm, Fri-Sat 5pm-midnight, brunch Sun noon-3:30pm ♿ Ⓥ

Flattop Grill (6, E4) $
Pan-Asian
The owners must have taken to heart the advice of famous stripper Gypsy

Rose Lee: 'You've gotta have a gimmick.' Here the hook is an all-you-can-eat, do-it-yourself stir-fry bar. You choose the ingredients, and the cooks fry it up and bring it to your table. It sounds awful but tastes good.
✉ 3714 Macomb St NW ☎ 244-0075
🚌 30, 32, 34, 35, 36
⏰ Sun-Thurs 11:30am-10:30pm, Fri-Sat 11:30am-11pm ♿ Ⓥ

Yanyu (6, E5) $$$
Pan-Asian
Chef Jessie Yan fuses Asian flavors in the firefly calamari, lily-bulb dumplings and vegetables with Malaysian curry, all graciously served in one of the city's more elegant spaces. If you have the time and money, try one of the tasting menus ($40-75), either vegetarian or carnivorous.
✉ 3435 Connecticut Ave NW ☎ 686-6968
Ⓜ Cleveland Park
🚌 L1, L2, L4 ⏰ Sun & Tues-Thurs 5:30-10:30pm, Fri-Sat 5:30-11pm Ⓥ

Smoking
Tobacco was the first cash crop here, and tobacco is still in evidence in restaurants all around town. A few places are nonsmoking, and a lot have designated nonsmoking sections, but generally speaking, in DC a smoker can enjoy a meal and a cig without having to trudge over to the bar or out to the sidewalk.

DOWNTOWN/FOGGY BOTTOM/WEST END

Andale (5, E9) $$
Mexican
Not a mere taquería, this spot makes a complex presentation of the contemporary flavors of Mexico. Everything here reflects a lot of thought, from the look of the dining room to the look of the *pato al mole negro* (duck with black mole sauce) on your plate.
✉ 401 7th St NW
☎ 783-3133
Ⓜ Archives/Navy Memorial, Gallery Pl/Chinatown ◷ lunch Mon-Sat 11:30am-3pm; dinner Mon-Thurs 5-10pm, Fri-Sat 5-11pm

Aroma (5, C3) $$
Indian
This neighborhood spot makes an easy stop for tandoori chicken, chicken kebabs with coriander and mint, and reliable renditions of familiar lamb and seafood dishes.
✉ 1919 I St NW
☎ 833-4700 Ⓜ Farragut West ◷ lunch Mon-Fri 11:30-2:30, Sat-Sun noon-2:30pm; dinner 5:30-10pm (to 10:30pm Fri-Sat) ♿ Ⓥ

Capitol Q (5, D9) $
Barbecue
You wouldn't expect to find the best barbecue in town in the middle of Chinatown, but here it is. All the classics – ribs, smoked turkey, beef brisket and sausages – come on white bread with sauces from hot to hotter. Even the complete lack of charm in the small space is an authentic small-town Texan touch.
✉ 707 H St NW
☎ 347-8392 Ⓜ Gallery Pl/Chinatown ◷ Mon-Thurs 11am-7pm, Fri 11am-8pm, Sat 11:30am-8pm

Daily Grill (5, B4) $$$
American
Come here for top-of-the-line American comfort food: steaks, chops, chicken and fish like you wish your mother made, with huge portions of all the best cuts. A good place for business, it's equally good for a meal alone after a tough day.
✉ 1200 18th St NW
☎ 822-5282 Ⓜ Farragut North, Dupont Circle ◷ Mon-Thurs 11:30am-11pm, Fri-Sat 11:30am-midnight, Sun 10am-11pm ♿ Ⓥ

Fado Irish Pub (5, D9) $
Irish
The fare here ranges from full-on Irish (Galway Bay mussels, Atlantic smoked salmon and an Irish take on shepherd's pie) to

Considering 'cue

American dishes with an Irish twist (chicken Caesar wraps in boxties – traditional potato pancakes).
✉ 808 7th St NW
☎ 789-0066
Ⓜ Gallery Pl/Chinatown ◷ 11:30am-2am

Full Kee (5, D10) $
Chinese
At the best dive in Chinatown, fill yourself for next to nothing with a simple noodle dish or gorge on a wondrous stir-fry. Better still, go for one of the rich, savory casseroles you won't find many other places, like eggplant and short ribs or pork and bean curd. No alcohol, no credit cards.
✉ 509 H St NW
☎ 371-2233
Ⓜ Gallery Pl/Chinatown ◷ 11am-1am (Fri-Sat to 3am) ♿ Ⓥ

Georgia Brown's (5, C6) $$$
Southern
Serious Southern cooking with an emphasis on savory Low Country dishes combines seafood from the Carolina coast with flavors from West Indies plantations. Try the Frogmore stew, which includes shrimp, corn and sausage. Georgia's is popular with the K St lobbying crowd, with black urban professionals and with anyone else who wonders just how good a plate of grits can get.
✉ 950 15th St NW
☎ 393-4499
Ⓜ McPherson Sq ◷ Mon-Thurs 11:30am-10:30pm, Fri 11:30am-11:30pm, Sat 5:30-11:30pm, Sun 11:30am-3pm & 5:30-10:30pm

Jaleo (5, E9) $$

Spanish

An anchor of the new Penn Quarter, this downtown institution serves hot and cold tapas for lunch, afternoon snacks or dinner.

✉ 480 7th St NW
☎ 628-7949 Ⓜ Gallery Pl/Chinatown, Archives/Navy Memorial ◷ Sun-Mon 11:30am-10pm, Tues-Thurs 11:30am-11:30pm, Fri-Sat 11:30am-10:30pm ♿ Ⓥ

Kaz Sushi Bistro (5, C4) $$

Japanese

Fusion with a difference, Kaz' cuisine takes you to Japan by way of France. Sample sushi and other Japanese dishes and a handful of specials with that *je ne sais quoi*.

✉ 1915 I St NW
☎ 530-5500 Ⓜ Farragut West ◷ lunch Mon-Fri 11:30am-2pm, dinner Mon-Sat 6-10pm Ⓥ

Kinkead's (5, D3) $$$$

American

The seafood arrives so fresh you can taste the sea. You'll get a flavor of lots of different places, inventively combined. Always sensational, Kinkead's is worth the hype.

✉ 2000 Pennsylvania Ave NW ☎ 296-7700

Ⓜ Foggy Bottom/GWU
◷ lunch 11:30am-2:30pm, dinner 5:30-10:30pm

Legal Sea Foods (5, C3) $$$

American

Those Bostonians have brought their winning formula of 'If it's not fresh, it's not legal' to the capital. Despite being an import, Legal serves some of the best chowder or fish you'll find anywhere in town.

✉ 2020 K St NW (also at 704 7th St NW)
☎ 496-1111 Ⓜ Farragut West ◷ Mon-Thurs 11am-10pm, Fri 11am-10:30pm, Sat 4-10:30pm, Sun 4-9pm ♿

Loeb's Deli Restaurant (5, C6) $

Jewish

The closest thing to a New York deli in DC offers the standards plus sidewalk seating that you won't find in the Big Apple.

✉ 832 15th St NW
☎ 783-9306
Ⓜ McPherson Sq
◷ Mon-Fri 6am-4:30pm ♿

Red Sage (5, E7) $$$

Modern American

Mark Miller began his career with famed chef Alice Waters in Berkeley,

California, before moving to Santa Fe and opening Coyote Café. He brought his personal fusion of New Mexican and New American cooking to town years ago. He still packs crowds into an aggressively ugly dining room; the food makes you forget your surroundings.

✉ 605 14th St NW
☎ 638-4444 Ⓜ Metro Center, McPherson Sq
◷ Mon-Sat 11:30am-11:30pm,
Sun 4:30-11pm Ⓥ

Sholl's Colonial Cafeteria (5, C3) $

American

Southerners love cafeterias, and Sholl's is one of the reasons for this abiding affair. For about the price of a Big Mac and an order of fries, enjoy comfort food like chopped steak with mashed potatoes or sweet potatoes. Save room for those Jell-O desserts rarely seen north of the Mason-Dixon Line.

✉ 1990 K St NW
☎ 296-3065 Ⓜ Farragut West, McPherson Sq ◷ Mon-Sat 7:30-10:30am, 11am-2:30pm & 4-8pm ♿

Vidalia (5, B3) $$$$

Modern American

Named for the home of those sweet Georgia onions, Vidalia is one of the top tickets in Washington for modern American cooking with a Southern edge. Formal without being stuffy, it's a favorite of the downtown power crowd.

✉ 1990 M St NW
☎ 659-1990 Ⓜ Farragut West ◷ lunch Mon-Fri 11:30-2:30pm; dinner Mon-Thurs 5:30-10pm, Fri-Sat 5:30-10:30pm

Southern Cooking

With all the hoopla over French and Ethiopian cuisine in DC, it's easy to forget that the chefs here do some serious regional cooking that's hard to find anywhere else in the world – English country fare with New World ingredients and African influences. Some favorite Southern cooking spots include **Georgia Brown's** (p. 79), the **Morrison-Clark Historic Inn & Restaurant** (p. 102), **Vidalia** (p. 80) and, of course, **Market Lunch** (p. 77).

DUPONT CIRCLE

Afterwords (4, C6) $
American
The food side of the Kramerbooks complex (the center of intelligent life in Dupont Circle), this café offers simple coffee shop fare – big breakfasts, light lunches and dinners featuring pastas, salads and sandwiches.
✉ 1517 Connecticut Ave NW ☎ 387-1400
Ⓜ Dupont Circle
🕐 Mon-Thurs 7:30am-1am, Fri 7:30am-Mon 1am ♿ V

Bistrot du Coin (4, C6) $$$
French
Could this be France? The sunny yellow room looks like the real thing, the waiters gargle their Rs, and what arrives on the plates smells and tastes just the way it should – bistro food, heavy on the meats, heavy on the rich sauces, with perfect frites and little salads on the side.
✉ 1738 Connecticut Ave NW ☎ 234-6969
Ⓜ Dupont Circle
🕐 Sun & Tues-Wed 11:30am-11pm, Thurs-Sat 11:30am-1am

City Lights of China (4, C6) $
Chinese
One of the places where Washingtonians learned to eat with chopsticks, City Lights still serves dependable Cantonese-oriented dishes and Peking duck in a set of cozy basement dining rooms.
✉ 1731 Connecticut Ave NW ☎ 265-6688
Ⓜ Dupont Circle
🕐 Mon-Thurs 11:30am-10:30pm, Fri 11:30am-11pm, Sat noon-11pm, Sun noon-10:30pm ♿ V

Johnny's Half Shell (5, A3) $$
American
Flavorful seafood comes from both near (Maryland crab cakes) and far (spicy file gumbo from New Orleans), with fish predominating on the short menu. A typical night features seafood stew, pan-roast cod or grilled rockfish, with some red meat on the menu if you've got an incorrigible in tow. Order oysters and clams from the raw bar.
✉ 2002 P St NW ☎ 296-2021
Ⓜ Dupont Circle
🕐 lunch 11:30am-5pm, dinner Mon-Thurs 5-10:30pm, Fri-Sat 5-11pm

Julia's Empanadas (5, B4) $
Latin American
Every country in Latin America makes its own version of the empanada (a turnover filled with meat or vegetables or both). Julia's little stands offer a delicious assortment of Chilean, chorizo and other varieties, perfect for snacking or an on-the-move meal. Try them here, in Adams-Morgan, Downtown and on U St.
✉ 1221 Connecticut Ave NW ☎ 861-8828
Ⓜ Dupont Circle
🕐 Mon-Wed 10am-10pm, Thurs-Fri 10am-2am, Sat 10am-7pm, Sun 10am-4pm ♿ V

Lauriol Plaza (4, C6) $$
Tex-Mex
The liveliest spot in Adams-Morgan offers a Californian version of Tex-Mex food, from lightly seasoned taco and enchilada plates to fancier seafood and meat dishes like grilled quail or Cuban-style pork. The huge sidewalk seating area and rooftop terrace are added draws, so expect a wait.
✉ 1835 18th St NW ☎ 387-0035
Ⓜ Dupont Circle 🚌 L2
🕐 11am-11pm (Fri-Sat to midnight) V

Levante's (5, A4) $$
Mediterranean
Gorgeous dishes from every corner of the Levant grace a space so elegant you'll never think of a Greek diner in the same way again. Turkish pides (pizza breads) from the wood-burning oven compete for attention with kebabs, kofte (meatballs) and chops off the grill. Salads, sandwiches

A Dupont Circle institution beckons.

Rick Gerharter

and baked dishes finish off the list.

✉ 1320 19th St NW
☎ 293-3244
Ⓜ Dupont Circle
🕐 Mon-Fri 11:30am-10pm, Sat noon-11pm, Sun noon-10pm ♿ Ⓥ

Mercury Grill
(4, C7) $$$
Modern American
There's a lot going on here, from the sidewalk outside to the overly busy pasta, chicken and fish dishes on your plate, but when it's all said and done, Mercury Grill offers probably the best food on the strip of 17th St that passes for Boystown in DC. Expect tasty fare, professional staff and a street scene that's divine.

✉ 1602 17th St NW
☎ 667-5937
Ⓜ Dupont Circle
🕐 Sun-Thurs 5:30-10:30pm, Fri-Sat 5:30-11pm, brunch Sun 11am-3pm

Nora (4, C6) $$$
Modern American
Nora is the queen of the Washington food scene. Like her Californian counterpart, Alice Waters, she's made her reputation serving food from local farmers and ranchers, usually organic and always fresh, and combining ingredients in new and interesting ways. The results may be uneven at times, but the

path to true culinary enlightenment is rarely direct.

✉ 2132 Florida Ave NW
☎ 462-5143
Ⓜ Dupont Circle
🕐 Mon-Thurs 6-10pm, Fri-Sat 6-10:30pm Ⓥ

Pizza Paradiso
(5, A3) $
Italian
You can spend up to $50 for an amazing prix fixe Italian meal from Peter Pastan at Obelisk, next door, or you can come here and spend a whole lot less for one of his deceptively simple pizzas or perfect panini. It just goes to show that your mother was right — good taste need not cost more.

✉ 2029 P St NW
☎ 223-1245
Ⓜ Dupont Circle
🕐 Mon-Thurs 11:30am-11pm, Fri 11:30am-midnight, Sat 11am-midnight, Sun noon-10pm ♿ Ⓥ

Raku (4, C6) $
Pan-Asian
Mark Miller (of Red Sage, p. 80) proves that he's no one-hit wonder with this pan-Asian diner. At Raku, Miller adds to his culinary repertoire with scrumptious sushi and succulent noodle dishes from Hong Kong and points Far East, served up in modish surroundings perfect for the

setting on a busy Dupont Circle corner.

✉ 1900 Q St NW
☎ 265-7528
Ⓜ Dupont Circle
🕐 11:30am-10pm (Fri-Sat to 11pm) Ⓥ

Teaism (4, C6) $
Teahouse
Rain or shine, the front court of Teaism is one of the loveliest spots in Washington, a Japanese garden that doubles as a place to savor the delicate sandwiches and snacks you'll find inside when you enter for one of the dozens of teas.

✉ 2009 R St NW (also at 800 Connecticut Ave NW & 400 8th St NW)
☎ 667-3827
Ⓜ Dupont Circle
🕐 Mon-Thurs 8am-11pm, Sat 9am-11pm, Sun 9am-10pm ♿ Ⓥ

Thaiphoon (4, C6) $$
Thai
The food doesn't always match the level of the sensational decor, but it's good enough to draw consistent crowds, particularly for seafood and vegetable dishes, which gives the place a buzz to match the tingles of Thai spices in the dishes.

✉ 2011 S St NW
☎ 667-3505
Ⓜ Dupont Circle
🕐 11:30am-10:30pm (Fri-Sat to 11pm) ♿ Ⓥ

Dinner for One
Eating at the counter is one of the best ways to deal with eating alone. There's usually enough light to read by and often a fellow solo patron nearby if you feel the urge to strike up a conversation. You'll find some of the best counters in Washington at **Ben's Chili Bowl** (p. 85), **Centre Café** (p. 76), **Daily Grill** (p. 79), **Johnny's Half Shell** (p. 81) and **Raku** (above).

Rick Gerharter

GEORGETOWN

Bangkok Bistro of Georgetown (2, D2) **$**
Thai
Don't be put off by the way-cool design of the room. The contemporary Thai food on the plates will satisfy most diners (though some may prefer less spice in the decor, more in the food).
✉ 3251 Prospect St NW ☎ 337-2424
Ⓜ Foggy Bottom/GWU
🚌 30, 32, 34, 35, 36, Georgetown shuttles
🕐 Mon-Thurs 11:30am-11pm, Fri 11:30am-midnight, Sat noon-midnight, Sun noon-11pm ♿ Ⓥ

Bistro Français (2, D3) **$$$**
French
And you thought no one served onion soup anymore. This traditional French bistro offers the same kind of French food that took America by storm in the 1960s, in a classic red-leather-booth setting. Enjoy that soup after midnight, like Les Halles in the old days.
✉ 3124-28 M St NW
☎ 338-3830 Ⓜ Foggy Bottom/GWU 🚌 30, 32, 34, 35, 36, Georgetown shuttles
🕐 11am-3am (Fri-Sat to 4am)

Booeymonger (2, D2) **$**
Sandwiches
Students, shoppers and office workers from the neighborhood line up at this dive for breakfast in the morning (mainly eggs and omelets) or inexpensive sandwiches in about every shape or size. Try the Philly cheese steak or the Patty

Hearst (Booeymonger's version of a club).
✉ 3265 Prospect St NW ☎ 333-4810
Ⓜ Foggy Bottom/GWU
🚌 30, 32, 34, 35, 36, Georgetown shuttles
🕐 Mon-Fri 7:30am-midnight, Sat-Sun 8am-midnight (breakfast served Mon-Fri to 11:30am, Sat to noon, Sun to 1pm) ♿ Ⓥ

Café Milano (2, D2) **$$$**
Italian
Italian food like you'd find in Italy draws foodies, fashionistas and the Georgetown lunch set, who nibble on the salads and the delicate pasta dishes or gorge on the fish and veal entrees that dominate the menu.
✉ 3251 Prospect St NW ☎ 333-6183
Ⓜ Foggy Bottom/GWU
🚌 30, 32, 34, 35, 36, Georgetown shuttles
🕐 11:30am-midnight (Thurs-Sat to 2am) Ⓥ

Citronelle (2, D4) **$$$$**
French
Michel Richard has brought his blend of Escoffier and Disney from Citrus in Los Angeles to the Latham Hotel. You'll see evidence of his training as a pastry chef in the shrimp wrapped in filo or his signature chocolate bar based on a Kit-Kat. Show up in your dressiest attire.
✉ 3000 M St NW
☎ 625-2150 Ⓜ Foggy Bottom/GWU 🚌 30, 32, 34, 35, 36, Georgetown shuttles 🕐 lunch Mon-Fri noon-2pm, dinner Sun-Thurs 6:30-10pm, Fri-Sat 6-10:30pm

Moby Dick House of Kebab (2, D3) **$**
Middle Eastern
The best kebab stand in the city started here and spread to five other locations in the metro area. Try the ground lamb, lamb bits, chicken or beef. Leave room for the savory rice or an Iranian side dish. There are some stools to sit at in store, or you can take away for a waterfront picnic.
✉ 1070 31st St NW
☎ 333-4400 Ⓜ Foggy Bottom/GWU 🚌 30, 32, 34, 35, 36, Georgetown shuttles 🕐 Sun-Thurs 11am-10pm, Fri 11am-4am, Sat noon-4am ♿ Ⓥ

Sidewalk dining in G-town

Neyla Mediterranean Grill (2, C2) **$$$**
Mediterranean
The food at this chic Lebanese restaurant reflects all the cultures of the Phoenician coast, from traditional mezza to French-inflected duck breast and confit to grilled Moroccan tuna.
✉ 3206 N St NW
☎ 333-6353 Ⓜ Foggy Bottom/GWU 🚌 30, 32, 34, 35, 36, Georgetown shuttles
🕐 5-11pm Ⓥ

Old Glory (2, D3) $

Barbecue

The great Memphis-style barbecue joint in town serves up ribs and pulled-pork sandwiches that are ready for prime time (in this case, prime time is the World Championship Barbecue Cooking Contest, held in Memphis every May).

✉ 3139 M St NW
☎ 337-3406 Ⓜ Foggy Bottom/GWU 🚌 30, 32, 34, 35, 36, Georgetown shuttles
🕒 11:30am-2am (Fri-Sat to 3am)

Peacock Cafe (2, D2) $$

Mediterranean-American

This bright space around from the Wisconsin Ave shops offers health food, smoothies and sandwiches alongside pastas and salads that reveal chef Maziar Farivar's Iranian heritage.

✉ 3251 Prospect St NW ☎ 625-2740
Ⓜ Foggy Bottom/GWU
🚌 30, 32, 34, 35, 36, Georgetown shuttles
🕒 Mon-Fri 11am-11pm, Sat-Sun 4-11pm, brunch Sat-Sun 9am-4pm ♿ Ⓥ

Prospects on Prospect (2, D2) $

Italian

A sensational selection of designer pizzas baked in a brick oven bears the signature of Maziar Farivar, chef of the Peacock Cafe down the block. He's come up with a great choice of salads to match, from classics like plum tomatoes and mozzarella to innovations like mango and pear with goat cheese and arugula.

✉ 3203 Prospect St NW ☎ 298-6800
Ⓜ Foggy Bottom/GWU
🚌 30, 32, 34, 35, 36, Georgetown shuttles
🕒 11:30am-10:30pm (Fri-Sat to 11:30pm)
♿ Ⓥ

Saigon Inn (2, D4) $

Vietnamese

This Vietnamese spot serves basic fare for very basic prices. It's great for pricey Georgetown.

✉ 2928 M St NW
☎ 337-5588 Ⓜ Foggy Bottom/GWU 🚌 30, 32, 34, 35, 36, Georgetown shuttles 🕒 11am-11pm (Fri-Sat to midnight) ♿

Sequoia (2, E4) $$$

Modern American

Best known for its river views, Sequoia puts together a nice scene on the plate, too. Look for a nice mix of grills and salads (try swordfish with Jamaican jerk spices or blackened catfish with okra hash).

✉ Washington Harbour, 3000 K St NW
☎ 944-4200 Ⓜ Foggy Bottom/GWU 🚌 30, 32, 34, 35, 36, Georgetown shuttles 🕒 Mon-Thurs 11:30am-midnight, Fri-Sat 11:30am-1am, Sun 10:30am-midnight
♿ Ⓥ

Kid Stuff

Thousands of school buses and millions of family wagons arrive in Washington every year, so most moderately priced restaurants are kid-friendly, with hours and menus for the under-16 set (look for the ♿ icon in our listings). When feeding wee ones, you can always head to food courts – quick, noisy and diverse, so all the young ones get what they want. **Union Station** (p. 37) and the **Ronald Reagan Building** (Pennsylvania Ave & 14th St NW; 5, F7) have the best ones in town. Other food courts to consider include those at **Georgetown Park Mall** (p. 58) and **Fashion Centre at Pentagon City** (p. 58).

Just in case you need your kid to be more hyperactive...

Rick Gerharter

U ST/14TH ST

Ben's Chili Bowl
(4, B8) **$**
Burgers & Hot Dogs
Ben's has been a fixture on U St since 1958, drawing Howard University professors, school kids and visitors from all parts of town for the chili dogs and chili burgers and the conversation at the lunch counter.
✉ **1213 U St NW**
☎ **667-0909**
Ⓜ U St/Cardozo 🚌 90, 92, 93, 96, 98 ⏱ Mon-Thurs 6am-2am, Fri-Sat 6am-4am, Sun noon-8pm ♿

Coppi's Pizza (4, B7) $
Italian
One of the pioneers in the rebirth of U St, this pizza parlor with a wood-fired oven serves pizzas and calzones made with a range of top-quality ingredients, some traditional and some less so. Brace yourself for the noise and the wait when it's crowded.
✉ **1414 U St NW**
☎ **319-7773**
Ⓜ U St/Cardozo 🚌 90, 92, 93, 96, 98
⏱ 5-11pm (Fri-Sat to midnight) ♿ **V**

U-Topia (4, B7) **$$**
World Food
Jamal Sahri came to U St to open an art gallery, but before long he changed his formula to 'Bar & Grill, Art & Eat.' The multicultural menu, featuring gumbos and couscous and pastas, mirrors the multiethnic neighborhood.
✉ **1418 U St NW**
☎ **483-7669** Ⓜ U St/ Cardozo 🚌 90, 92, 93, 96, 98 ⏱ Mon-Fri 11am-2am, Sat 5pm-3am, Sun 11:30am-2am ♿ **V**

WATERFRONT

Captain White's Seafood City (5, K8) $
Seafood
Get super-fresh spicy shrimp, clam chowder, Maryland crab soup and raw shellfish at this seafood stand, almost under the 14th St bridge..
✉ **Maine Ave Fish Market** ☎ **484-2722**

Ⓜ **Waterfront**
⏱ 7:30am-8:30pm ♿

Phillips Flagship Restaurant (5, K8) $$
Seafood
This enormous barn of a place is perched on the waterfront overlooking the placid Washington Channel. Like its brethren

establishments on the docks of Boston, New York and San Francisco, Phillips always offers fish that's fresh, if not particularly exceptional.
✉ **900 Water St SW**
☎ **488-8518** Ⓜ Waterfront ⏱ Mon-Fri 11am-10pm, Sat-Sun 10am-11pm ♿

WOODLEY PARK

Jandara (4, A5) $
Thai
This comfortable neighborhood spot serves familiar Thai foods to a mix of locals and visitors.
✉ **2606 Connecticut Ave NW** ☎ **387-8876**
Ⓜ Woodley Park/Zoo
⏱ 11:30am-10:30pm (Fri-Sat to 1am) ♿ **V**

New Heights
(4, A5) **$$$**
Fusion
New Heights is the excep-

tion to the rule that fusion means confusion. Yes, there's a juxtaposition of diverse food and flavors (eg, risotto with Virginia ham, quinoa dumplings with goat cheese and black bean pâté). But it works here year after year, outlasting would-be competitors.
✉ **2317 Calvert St NW**
☎ **234-4110** Ⓜ Woodley Park/Zoo ⏱ 5:30-10pm (Fri-Sat to 11pm), brunch Sun 11am-2:30pm **V**

Woodley Cafe
(4, A5) **$**
American
This glorified coffee shop is a great place to tuck into a sandwich or meatloaf while you people watch or catch the game on the big TV.
✉ **2619 Connecticut Ave NW** ☎ **332-5773**
Ⓜ Woodley Park/Zoo
⏱ Mon-Thurs 11am-11:30pm, Fri 11am-midnight, Sat 9am-midnight, Sun 9am-11:30pm ♿ **V**

entitlement

There's a lot more nightlife in Washington than you'd expect from a city of only half a million people. But start with the proposition that the District is 'downtown' for almost four million people, add to the mix tens of thousands of college students and tens of thousands of post-college types with jobs on Capitol Hill, then pile on thousands more visitors from out of town and do the math. Whatever your interests, there's something waiting for you during your night on the town.

Listings

For the latest information on who's doing what where, check the entertainment pages of the *Washington City Paper*, the free alternative paper that hits the streets every Thursday. The entertainment coverage in the *Washington Post* is good, though limited by its need to cover the entire metro area.

If you're looking for news on the gay and lesbian hot spots, get a copy of the *Washington Blade*, distributed weekly in most of the neighborhoods from Capitol Hill to Rock Creek Park.

Where you go is up to you. **Georgetown** hums with college-kid stuff and a couple of joints that survived older partygoers' move east. **Dupont Circle** and **Adams-Morgan** stay alive late into the night, too, as diners from the neighborhoods' restaurants make their way into the nearby bars and clubs. Their action spills into the **New U and 14th St**, now home to lounges and dance and rock clubs. A set of huge dance spots has colonized **Downtown**; the more low-key scene in **Capitol Hill** revolves around a series of no-host cocktail parties at the local bars.

Rick Gerharter

Daytime entertainment is free in Dupont Circle.

SPECIAL EVENTS

January *Presidential Inauguration* – Jan 20 every 4th year; balls, receptions and the swearing-in at the Capitol

February *Black History Month* – all month; special displays and exhibits all across town

President's Day – 3rd Mon; celebrations at Mount Vernon and the Lincoln Memorial

March *St Patrick's Day* – Mar 17; parade of Irish Americans down Constitution Ave followed by drinking all around town

Smithsonian Kite Festival – last Sat; kites of every description in the skies around the Washington Monument

Cherry Blossom Festival – last week of Mar & 1st week of Apr; culture and arts fest building up to a big parade

April *Easter Egg Roll* – Easter Mon; festivities for kids ages 3 to 6 on the south lawn of the White House (see picture below)

FilmFest DC – last week of Apr & 1st week of May; film screenings all around town, including the Kennedy Center

May *Memorial Day* – last Mon; wreaths laid at Arlington National Cemetery

June *Capital Pride* – early June; parade on the Mall and special events around town

Smithsonian Folklife Festival – 10 days leading up to Jul 4; a festival on the Mall featuring music, food and cultural events from around the world

July *Independence Day* – Jul 4; free concerts and fireworks on the Mall, a reading of the Declaration of Independence on the steps of the National Archives

September *DC Blues Festival* – early Sept; top local acts at Carter Barron Amphitheater in Rock Creek Park

Adams-Morgan Days – mid-Sept; DC's biggest neighborhood festival, on 18th St NW

October *Marine Corps Marathon* – last weekend; run to the Iwo Jima Memorial through DC

Gay & Lesbian Film Festival – mid-month at Lincoln Theater in the New U District

November *Veterans Day* – Nov 11; special memorial services at Arlington National Cemetery and the Vietnam Veterans Memorial

December *Kennedy Center Holiday Celebration* – all month; free music ranging from gospel performances to a sing-along *Messiah*

National Christmas Tree & Menorah Lighting – 2nd Thurs; lighting ceremony on the Ellipse, with the president doing the honors

Mark E Gibson

BARS & PUBS

Brickskeller (4, C6)

Over 700 beers (purportedly the largest selection in the world) give this huge saloon the feel of an overgrown frat house. Make your choices, then order a burger as ballast and have a good time.

✉ 1523 22nd St NW
☎ 293-1885 e www.thebrickskeller.com
Ⓜ Dupont Circle
⏰ Mon-Thurs 11:30am-2am, Fri 11:30am-3am, Sat 6pm-3am, Sun 6pm-2am

Bullfeathers (5, J14)

If the Tune Inn (p. 77) is too laid-back for your tastes, come here for a drink and some atmosphere after hours on Capitol Hill. The crowd runs to Hill types, the conversation to politics.

✉ 410 1st St SE
☎ 543-5005 Ⓜ Capitol South ⏰ Mon-Sat 11am-10:30pm, Sun 10:30am-9pm

Capitol City Brewing Company (5, C8)

This brewpub in a historic office building across from the Convention Center gets busy after work, when crowds come to refuel with pub food and to unwind with the four or five microbrews on tap.

✉ 1100 New York Ave NW (also at 2 Massachusetts Ave NW, across from Union Station)
☎ 628-2222 e www.capcitybrew.com
Ⓜ Metro Center
⏰ Mon-Sat 11am-1:30am, Sun 11am-midnight

Chi-Cha Lounge

(4, B7) Don't wear your suit or tie to this lounge that redefines 'comfortable,' with big stuffed sofas and chairs to sink into and live Latin jazz or recorded sounds that get you going without getting in your way. Add tapas and drinks stemming from owner Mauricio Fraga-Rosenfeld's roots back in Ecuador, and you won't want to leave.

✉ 1624 U St NW
☎ 234-8400 Ⓜ U St/Cardozo 🚌 90, 92 93, 94, 96, U-Link

⏰ 5:30pm-1:30am (Fri-Sat to 2:30am)

Clyde's of Georgetown (2, D2)

A pioneer in the neighborhood, the first serious saloon in Georgetown has also blazed new trails in combining good food with good drinks. It makes for a nice change of pace from the college-kid spots elsewhere in the area.

✉ 3236 M St NW
☎ 333-9180 Ⓜ Foggy Bottom/GWU 🚌 30, 32, 34, 35, 36, Georgetown shuttles ⏰ Mon-Thurs 11:30am-2am, Fri 11:30am-3am, Sat 10am-3am, Sun 9am-2am

Dragonfly (5, B4)

The people who run the 18th St Lounge (below) and Red (p. 20) bring you this restaurant/lounge with an all-white color scheme and electronic music from everywhere. Wash down your sushi with lots of martinis and cosmos.

✉ 1215 Connecticut Ave NW ☎ 331-1775
Ⓜ Dupont Circle
⏰ Mon-Thurs 5pm-1am, Fri 5:30pm-1:45am, Sat 6pm-1:45am, Sun 6pm-12:45am

Kelly's Irish Times

(5, E13) On Friday and Saturday, college kids and young staffers from the Hill meet to blend at one of the city's great pick-up spots. The live Irish music (Thursday to Saturday) would be an added draw, were that necessary.

✉ 14 F St NW ☎ 543-5433 Ⓜ Union Station

On the Town Alone

There's no need to hide in your hotel room watching CNN if you find yourself in Washington alone. You can enjoy a comfortable meal by yourself in a number of places (see 'Dinner for One,' p. 82). Single tickets are frequently easy to come by for concerts or theater shows. For solo drinking and lounging, look on this page for **Kelly's Irish Times**, **Capitol City Brewing Company** and the **Chi-Cha Lounge**; or try **Tryst** (2459 18th St NW; 3, C2; ☎ 232-5500), a coffeehouse and bar in Adams-Morgan; or **Champions** (1206 Wisconsin Ave NW; 2, D3; ☎ 965-4005), a Georgetown bar with TVs tuned to sports.

🕐 11am-1:30am
(Fri-Sat to 2:30am)

Millie & Al's (3, C2)
In a neighborhood filled with spots evoking Istanbul or Addis Ababa, this small-town US honky-tonk bar stands out. Like any good dive in West Virginia or West Texas, it's about downing shots and beers with your buds while you listen to music, watch the tube or scarf down a pizza.
✉ 2440 18th St NW
☎ 387-8131
Ⓜ Woodley Park/Zoo
🚌 90, 92, 93, 96, 98, L2, U-Link 🕐 4pm-2am
(Fri-Sat to 3am)

Republic Gardens
(4, B8) This chic spot for the black urban professional

crowd gets particularly busy on Wednesday (aka 'Singles Night'). Have a meal in the restaurant, watch a game at the sports bar or take a spin on the dance floor as the mood and the moment take you.
✉ 1355 U St NW
☎ 232-2710 Ⓜ U St/Cardozo 🚌 90, 92, 93, 96, 98, U-Link
🕐 Wed-Thurs 5pm-2am, Fri 5pm-3am, Sat 9pm-3am

Stetson's Famous Bar & Restaurant (4, B7)
'Famous' might be pushing things, but Stetson's can lay claim to fame as the neighborhood bar for the New U. It's basic – the pool table and the jukebox are the primary amenities –

and comfortable, with good burgers and frequent happy hours.
✉ 1610 U St NW
☎ 667-6295 Ⓜ U St/Cardozo 🚌 90, 92, 93, 96, 98, U-Link
🕐 4:30pm-2am

Beverages 'n' botany

DANCE CLUBS

Club Zei (5, C6)
This big warehouse dance club takes its looks from New York, but its crowd is homegrown: lots of students Thursday and Friday (when the minimum age drops to 18), older 20-somethings and even 30-somethings on Saturday. No sneakers or athletic gear.
✉ 1415 Zei Alley
(south of I St NW btw 14th & 15th Sts)
☎ 842-2445
Ⓜ McPherson Sq
🕐 Thurs-Sat 10pm-2am
💲 Thurs $10;
Fri-Sat $12

DC Live (5, E9)
This old converted department store claims to be the largest club in town: it holds four full floors that accommodate 2500 nightlifers. In a city of

white clubs and black clubs, it tries to appeal to everyone with a mixture of hip-hop, reggae and rhythm and blues. No jeans, no athletic shoes. Ages 18 and older allowed.
✉ 932 F St NW
☎ 347-7200 Ⓜ Gallery Pl/Chinatown, Metro Center 🕐 Wed 10pm-2am, Fri 5pm-3am, Sat 10pm-4am, Sun 10pm-3am 💲 varies

18th St Lounge (5, B4)
Eric Hilton and Rob Garza, better known as Thievery Corporation, have put together a mix of lively but mellow lounge sounds drawn from Brazil, the Caribbean and electronica sources everywhere. There's no sign on the door and no assurance that you'll get in, but if

you can deal with this attitude, go for it.
✉ 1212 18th St NW
☎ 466-3922
Ⓜ Dupont Circle
🕐 Tues-Wed 9:30pm-2am, Thurs 5:30pm-3am, Fri 3pm-3am, Sat 9:30pm-3am 💲 usually under $10

Habana Village (3, C2)
You don't have to be Latin to enjoy the salsa, the mambo or the merengue. You don't even have to dance. Downstairs music includes live Latin bands Sunday to Tuesday; they complement the sexy shaking on the floor upstairs.
✉ 1834 Columbia Rd NW ☎ 462-6310
Ⓜ Woodley Park/Zoo
🚌 42, L2, U-Link
🕐 7:30pm-2:30am
💲 downstairs free, upstairs cover varies

Heaven & Hell (3, D3)

In Heaven (upstairs), dance to disco, techno, retro or Goth/industrial. In Hell (downstairs), play pool and drink beer in a frat-house atmosphere. It's your night, so you choose.

✉ **2327 18th St NW**
☎ **667-4355** Ⓜ **Dupont Circle** 🚌 **L2** ⏲ **7:30pm-2am (Fri-Sat to 3am)**
⑤ **$5**

Platinum (5, E9)

The new kid on the downtown club block, Platinum is smaller, sleeker and dressier than DC Live, across the street. There's a VIP room, but you won't have to use it to feel like a VIP. No jeans, no athletic shoes.

✉ **915 F St NW**
☎ **393-3555** Ⓜ **Gallery Pl/Metro Center**
⏲ **Thurs-Sat 10pm-3am, Sun 9pm-2:30am**
⑤ **$10; $15 after midnight Sat**

Polly Esther's (5, E8)

Everybody claims to hate the 1970s, but local cabbies will confirm that every night a crowd rushes in to Polly Esther's, where disco never died. You won't need bad hair or a Nic-Nic shirt to fit into the retro surroundings,

It's no New York, but DC is still a town of fly threads.

just a little rhythm to follow that beat. Ages 18 and older allowed Thursday.

✉ **605 12th St NW**
☎ **737-1970** Ⓜ **Metro Center** ⏲ **Thurs 9pm-2am, Fri-Sat 8pm-3am**
⑤ **Thurs $5, Fri $8, Sat $10**

Red (5, B4)

A young, mixed crowd (gay and straight, black and white) gets going post-midnight at this after-hours club run by the people from the 18th St Lounge.

✉ **1802 Jefferson Pl NW** ☎ **466-3475**

Ⓜ **Dupont Circle**
⏲ **Wed-Sat 10pm-3am**
⑤ **varies**

The Ritz (5, E9)

One of the big clubs that have sprung up Downtown, this one sprawls across three dance floors, a lounge and a couple of bars featuring sounds from jazz to hip-hop for a largely 'buppie' (black urban professional) crowd. Wear proper attire.

✉ **919 E St NW**
☎ **638-2582** Ⓜ **Gallery Pl/Chinatown, Metro Center** ⏲ **Fri 10pm-10am, Sat 9pm-9am**
⑤ **varies**

State of the Union

(4, B7) Crowds converge nightly on 14th and U to an intoxicating mix of house, jungle and hip-hop. Live bands play five nights a week in the front room.

✉ **1357 U St NW**
☎ **588-8926** Ⓜ **U St/Cardozo** 🚌 **90, 92, 93, 94, 96, U-Link** ⏲ **Mon-Thurs 5pm-2am, Fri-Sat 5pm-3am, Sun 6pm-2am** ⑤ **$5-7; free Tues and before 8:30pm**

Going Go-Go

No, it's not girls in cages – go-go is DC's unique brand of percussion-driven dance. In the mid-'70s, Chuck Brown (the 'godfather of go-go') mixed disco with funk and syncopated Afro-Latin rhythms for an infectiously danceable combination. The unmistakable beat, with loud brass and bass drums and audience call-and-response ('Are you ready to go?' 'Hell, no!') remains popular.

Look in the *City Paper* or at Ⓔ members.tripod.com/~kid_mysfit/gogo.html. Wander the streets downtown to hear the beat on pots, pans and assorted paraphernalia.

– Laura Harger & Vivek Waglé

THEATER & COMEDY

Arena Stage (4, G9)
The most highly regarded theater company in the city was the first theater outside New York City to win a Tony Award. Arena produces new work and revives recent work on three stages at its modern complex on the Washington Channel.
✉ **1101 6th St SW**
☎ **488-3300** e **www .arenastage.org**
Ⓜ **Waterfront** Ⓢ **$30-45; discounts for those under age 25** ♿

Capitol Steps (5, F7)
Made up of former and present congressional staff people, this group has entertained fans across the country with their amusing musical takes on Washington life, sometimes broadcast on National Public Radio.
✉ **Ronald Reagan Trade Center, 1300 Pennsylvania Ave NW**
☎ **703-573-7328**
Ⓜ **Federal Triangle**
Ⓢ **$31.50/29.50**

The Improv (5, B4)
The only real comedy club in the District, this branch of The Improv in New York usually presents middle-name or big-name acts like Rita Rudner, Bobby Slayton or Tony Rock.
✉ **1140 Connecticut Ave NW** ☎ **296-7008**
e **www.dcimprov.com**
Ⓜ **Farragut North**
🕐 **Sun-Thurs 8:30pm, Fri-Sat 8 & 10:30pm**
Ⓢ **$10-25 & 2-item (food or drink) minimum**

National Theatre
(5, E7) Brought back from the dead to house traveling Broadway shows, this old theater also offers free performances by local artists on Monday, free performances for children on Saturday afternoon and free movies Monday evening in summer.
✉ **1321 Pennsylvania Ave NW** ☎ **628-6161**
e **www.national theatre.org** Ⓜ **Federal Triangle, Metro Center** Ⓢ **$15-75** ♿

Sign at Ford's Theatre

The Shakespeare Theatre (5, E9)
TST produces five plays every year, some by the Bard himself, others from theatrical masters as ancient as Euripides or as modern as Tennessee Williams.
✉ **450 7th St NW**
☎ **547-1122** e **www .shakespearedc.org**

Ⓜ **Archives/Navy Memorial, Gallery Pl/ Chinatown** Ⓢ **$14-56** ♿

Studio Theatre (5, A3)
Perhaps the best small theater company in the District, the Studio houses two 200-seat spaces in an old automobile dealership that survived the 1968 riots. The group's contemporary material comes from playwrights Samuel Beckett, David Mamet, AR Gurney and Eve Ensler.
✉ **1333 P St NW**
☎ **332-3300** e **www .studiotheatre.org**
🚌 **52, 53, 54, G2**
Ⓢ **$20-40** ♿

Warner Theater
(5, E7) A Roaring Twenties movie palace restored and converted to an 1800-seat theater, the Warner welcomes the Washington Ballet's *Nutcracker* every Christmas and hosts everything from high-culture theater and dance shows to lowlife comedians.
✉ **1299 Pennsylvania Ave NW** ☎ **783-4000**
e **www.warner theatre.org** Ⓜ **Federal Triangle, Metro Center** Ⓢ **$25-55** ♿

Theater at the Kennedy Center
The Kennedy Center includes three stages dedicated to theater, aside from the concert hall and the opera house. The **Eisenhower Theater** usually produces dramatic plays while the **Terrace Theater** presents plays, recitals and experimental work. The **Theatre Lab** focuses on young people in its work. If all that's not enough for you, the **Millennium Stage** presents free performances of just about everything, including theater works, every evening at 6:30pm.

CINEMAS

Not a prime destination for film buffs, the entire District contains relatively few commercial multiplexes and even fewer art-house options. If you're looking for something more arcane than the latest date flick, you'll need to check the fine print in the *Washington City Paper*.

AMC Union Station 9
(5, E14) Built in the enormous storage rooms behind the Union Station terminal, this multiplex with a difference contains a range of theaters large and small, with screens that run the gamut from not-much-bigger-than-your-TV to panoramic. Parking and food in the Union Station terminal complete the package.
✉ Union Station, 50 Massachusetts Ave NE
☎ 998-4262 e www.amctheaters.com
Ⓜ Union Station ♿

American Film Institute Theater
(4, E5) A serious place to see serious films, the AFI screens about 800 movies a year, mostly one-night stands. The 224-seat theater features stadium seating and a large screen. Eat before you arrive – there's no snack bar and (alas) no popcorn.
✉ Kennedy Center, 2700 F St NW ☎ 785-4600 e www.afi.com
Ⓜ Foggy Bottom/GWU
🚌 Kennedy Center shuttles
$ $6.50/5.50 ♿

Loews Cineplex Dupont Circle 5
(5, A4) With five screens, one of the two multiplexes in Dupont Circle (the other is the Janus Cineplex 3, at Connecticut Ave & Hillyer Pl) offers a larger selection than its neighbor up the street.
✉ 1350 19th St NW
☎ 333-3456 e www.loewscineplex.com
Ⓜ Dupont Circle ♿

Loews Uptown (6, E5)
Its 1500 seats make this the largest theater in town and, thus, the place to see a big-screen feature like a re-release of *Star Wars* or *Lawrence of Arabia*.
✉ 3426 Connecticut Ave NW ☎ 966-4500
e www.loewscineplex.com
Ⓜ Cleveland Park ♿

Visions Cinema Bistro Lounge (4, C6)
The one place in town to see an independent film aside from the AFI or a college campus, Visions includes two screening rooms and a café serving snacks from the Lebanese taverna and desserts from all over. Stop in at the lounge in front, which features a bar, coffee bar and live music.
✉ 1927 Florida Ave NW ☎ 667-0090
e www.visionsdc.com
Ⓜ Dupont Circle 🚌 42
$ $10/8/6 ♿

Stay away if possessed: the famous Exorcist *steps*

Rick Gerharter

CLASSICAL MUSIC, DANCE & OPERA

National Symphony Orchestra (4, E5)
Directed by Leonard Slatkin, the National Symphony Orchestra presents work by contemporary American composers and European masters in the Kennedy Center from September to June. During the summer, you can catch free concerts outdoors at the Carter Barron Amphitheater in Rock Creek Park, or at the US Capitol on Memorial Day, Independence Day and Labor Day weekends.
✉ Kennedy Center, 2700 F St NW
☎ 416-8100 e www .kennedy-center.org
Ⓜ Foggy Bottom/GWU
◷ box office Mon-Sat 10am-9pm, Sun noon-9pm ⑤ $19-69
♿ some concerts for children

Washington Ballet
(4, E5) The Washington Ballet puts on a season of modern and classical works lasting from September to May, with performances at the Kennedy Center, the Warner Theater and George Mason University, in Virginia. The annual performance of The Nutcracker runs for two weeks in December (see the Warner Theater description, p. 91).
✉ Kennedy Center, 2700 F St NW; Warner Theater, 1299 Pennsylvania Ave NW
☎ 467-4600 e www .washingtonballet.org
Ⓜ Kennedy Center: Foggy Bottom/GWU; Warner Theater: Federal Triangle ♿

Washington Chamber Symphony
(4, E5) Known for its family and children's programs, this small independent symphony performs at the Kennedy Center and the Corcoran Gallery (p. 34).
✉ Kennedy Center, 2700 F St NW ☎ 452-1321 e www.wc symphony.org
Ⓜ Foggy Bottom/GWU
⑤ $22-50 ♿

Washington Opera
(4, E5) Directed by world-famous tenor Placido Domingo, this highly regarded company puts on about eight operas a year from September to November and from March to June. The 2001-2002 season included such works as Carmen, Madame Butterfly and Of Mice and Men.
✉ Kennedy Center, 2700 F St NW ☎ 295-2400 e www.dc -opera.org Ⓜ Foggy Bottom/GWU ◷ box office June-Aug Mon-Fri 10am-5pm; Sept-May Mon-Fri 10am-7pm, Sat noon-5:30pm; other times 90mins prior to performances ⑤ $60-140

Wolf Trap Opera Company (6, E1)
This independent opera company has dedicated itself to finding and training singers, coaches and directors from around the country and world. It accomplishes this through its artists-in-residence program, which takes place every summer. The company presents three productions a year, in both the verdant outdoor expanse of the Filene Center and the intimate space of the Barns (see 'Wolf Trap Farm,' below).
✉ 1624 Trap Road, Vienna, VA ☎ 703-255-1935 e www .wolf-trap.org
Ⓜ Vienna (then shuttle to Wolf Trap Farm)
⑤ $16-48 ♿

Wolf Trap Farm
Thirty years ago, Catherine Filene Shouse donated her 130-acre farm near Dulles airport to the National Park Service to create the country's first national party for the performing arts. Today, Wolf Trap Farm presents dance, theater and music year-round, both outdoors at the 7000-seat **Filene Center** and indoors at the 325-seat **Barns at Wolf Trap**. It also hosts outdoors children's programs at the **Theater-in-the-Woods**. Half the seating at the Filene Center is reserved, but the other half is first-come, first-served. Check the schedule on the e www.wolf-trap.org; buy tickets online or on the phone from tickets.com (☎ 800-955-5566) and pack your picnic basket.

ROCK, JAZZ & BLUES

Black Cat (4, B7)

The new home of indie rock in the New U features a main stage, a back stage, and the ground-floor Red Room lounge, where you can eat, drink or hang without a cover charge if the live music and after-show dancing upstairs don't appeal.

✉ 1811 14th St NW ☎ 667-7960 Ⓜ U St/Cardozo 🚌 52, 53, 54, 90, 92, 93, 94, 96, 98, U-Link ⏰ Sun-Thurs 8pm-2am, Fri-Sat 7pm-3am Ⓢ $3-20

Blues Alley (2, D3)

The gold standard of jazz clubs in the District, Blues Alley is where you go to see Wynton Marsalis or Nancy Wilson. The prices are steep, but the room is small (only 40 tables) and the acoustics and sightlines are sensational.

✉ 1073 Wisconsin Ave NW ☎ 337-4141 Ⓜ Foggy Bottom/GWU 🚌 30, 32, 34, 35, 36, Georgetown shuttles ⏰ 6pm-12:30am Ⓢ $14-50 cover & $7 minimum drinks or food, students half-price; 10pm shows Sun-Thurs

Columbia Station

(3, D3) At this easygoing neighborhood jazz joint, you can get a bite to eat, something to drink and something to listen to any night of the week.

✉ 2325 18th St NW ☎ 462-6040 Ⓜ Woodley Park/Zoo 🚌 90, 92, 93, 94, 96, 98, L2, U-Link ⏰ 11:30am-2am (Fri-Sat to 5am); shows 9:30pm Ⓢ 1-item minimum

The Dubliner (5, E13)

This Capitol Hill restaurant turns into a music hall near dinnertime, with live Irish or Celtic bands every evening. There's no cover charge, but you'll want to be spending some money on the food or the drink, so plan ahead.

✉ 540 N Capitol St ☎ 737-3773 ℮ www.pphotel.com Ⓜ Union Station ⏰ shows Mon-Sat 9pm, Sat 7pm Ⓢ free

Galaxy Hut (4, F1)

An alternative site for alternative rock near the Clarendon Metro station, this tiny spot somehow manages to squeeze in a vegetarian kitchen, a stage and a band of regular customers who come for the bands, for the beers or for 'Hump Night' on Wednesday, when anyone can DJ.

✉ 2711 Wilson Blvd, Arlington, VA ☎ 703-525-8646 ℮ www.galaxyhut.com Ⓜ Clarendon ⏰ Mon-Fri 5pm-2am, Sat-Sun 7pm-2am Ⓢ free

Grog & Tankard

(4, B3) Local bands play all the old rock 'n' roll favorites for a college and an I-miss-college crowd at this neighborhood joint at the far north end of Georgetown.

✉ 2408 Wisconsin Ave NW ☎ 333-3184 🚌 30, 32, 34, 35, 36 ⏰ Mon-Sat 6pm-2am Ⓢ $5

Madam's Organ Restaurant & Bar

(3, C2) 'Where the beautiful people go to get ugly,' this extremely popular Adams-Morgan joint features every shade of the blues, from blues to bluegrass to rhythm and blues every night of the week. To find the place, just look for the 25ft-tall (8m) mural of the busty Madam on the side of the building.

✉ 2461 18th St NW ☎ 667-5370 ℮ www.madamsorgan.com Ⓜ Woodley Park/Zoo 🚌 90, 92, 93, 94, 96, 98, L2, U-Link ⏰ 5pm-2am (Fri-Sat to 3am); shows Sun-Thurs 9pm, Fri-Sat 10pm Ⓢ $1-7

Rules of the Road

The drinking age in DC is 21, and with all the students in town it's strictly enforced. The big clubs often admit people between 18 and 21 at least a couple of nights a week, giving wristbands to the under-21s or vice versa to avoid problems at the bars. We've tried to note which days are which, but the days can change, so call ahead if you can. Drinking and driving, or driving under the influence of drugs, is a very bad idea. At the very least, you will get a tour of the District's lockups, which is on anyone's list of the low-lights of Washington.

Metro Cafe (4, C7)

The Metro made its reputation with indie rock and hip-hop shows, but it also holds dance nights, comedy nights and hard-to-classify performances, earning an accolade from the *Post* as 'the Swiss Army knife of local clubs.'

✉ 1522 14th St NW
☎ 588-9118 e www
.metrocafe.net 🚌 52,
53, 54, G2 ⏰ 7pm-2am
(Fri-Sat to 3am)

The Nation (4, G10)

The old Capitol Ballroom is a serious rock concert venue that doubles as a dance club, particularly Saturday night, when buffed gay boys flock in for 'Velvet Nation.' Hang out in the bars, lounges and patio if you need a break. The neighborhood is rough, so cab it.

✉ 1015 Half St SE
☎ 554-1500 ⏰ shows
weeknights, dance parties weekends ⓢ varies

9:30 Club (4, B8)

What do George Clinton, Natalie Merchant and Dwight Yoakam have in common? They're all recent headliners at the 9:30 Club – the most electric, most eclectic music hall in the District, housed in the old WUST Radio Music Hall near Howard University.

✉ 815 V St NW
☎ 393-0930 e www
.930.com Ⓜ U St/
Cardozo ⏰ hrs vary
ⓢ $5-45

Takoma Station Tavern (6, D6)

This low-key neighborhood joint near the Takoma Metro station showcases local acts and draws a heavily professional crowd that takes music seriously.

The Early Duke

'My road runs from Ward's Place to my grandmother's at Twentieth and R, to Seatan Street, around to Eighth Street, back up to T Street, through LeDroit Park to Sherman Avenue,' wrote DC's most famous musical son, Edward Kennedy Ellington (1899-1974), describing his childhood in the Shaw district. As a tot, Ellington purportedly first tackled the keyboard under a teacher named Mrs Clinkscales, but he honed his chops by listening to local ragtime pianists like Doc Perry, Louis Thomas and Louis Brown in Shaw, which at the time hosted one of the country's finest black arts scenes. His first composition, written at age 16, was 'Soda Fountain Rag.' The handsome, suave young Duke played hops and cabarets all over black Washington before decamping for New York in 1923.

– *Laura Harger*

Rick Gerharter

It's an anomaly for the District but perfect for the People's Republic of Takoma Park, across the street in Maryland.

✉ 6914 4th St NW
☎ 829-1999 e www
.takomastation.com
Ⓜ Takoma ⏰ 4pm-
2am ⓢ $5-20

GAY & LESBIAN WASHINGTON

Clubs line the commercial strips along P St west of Dupont Circle (aka 'the Circle') and 17th St between P and R Sts, but gay nightspots have also dispersed elsewhere in town, from Downtown to Capitol Hill to Southeast DC near the Navy Yard.

Actor's Theatre of Washington (4, C7)

This neighborhood theater at the Playbill Cafe presents works of gay and lesbian interest, ranging from funny stuff like Paul Rudnick's *The Most Fabulous Story Ever Told* to more serious fare like the drama *Sticks & Bones*.

✉ 1409 14th St NW
☎ 800-494-8497
🚌 G2 ⏱ Thurs-Fri 8pm, Sat 8 & 10:30pm, Sun 7pm 💲 $17

Badlands (5, A2)

The best place for dancing in Dupont Circle is wall-to-wall boys on Friday, the busiest night of the week. Thursday, it's one of the few spots in town where the 18-21 set can go dancing.

✉ 1415 22nd St NW
☎ 296-0505 Ⓜ Dupont Circle 🚌 G2 ⏱ Thurs-Sat 9pm-4am, Sun 9pm-2am 💲 $4; $8 after 10pm

Club Chaos (4, C7)

'Latin Night' on Thursday draws boys and girls for salsa and merengue; other nights, comedy and drag shows attracts different kinds of crowds to this bar/club tucked in a basement on the 17th St strip.

✉ 1603 17th St NW
☎ 232-4141
Ⓜ Dupont Circle 🚌 G2
⏱ 5pm-2am (Fri-Sat to 3am) 💲 free

DC Eagle (5, C10)

The bright klieg lights that were installed on the back porch on the 2nd floor didn't cut down on the cruising in the only leather bar in town. The neighborhood empties out after dark (at least until the new convention center nearby is finished), so drive or take a taxi.

✉ 639 New York Ave NW ☎ 347-6025
⏱ 4pm-2am (Fri-Sat to 3am) 💲 free

Hung Jury (5, D4)

The bar may be old (some say it's the oldest lesbian bar in the country), but the crowd tends to be young and hip (ages 18 and over are allowed). Come to play pool, hang out in the lounge or hit the dance floor.

✉ 1819 H St NW, behind Diplomat Garage ☎ 785-8181
Ⓜ Farragut West
⏱ Fri 10pm-3am, Sat 9pm-3am 💲 $10

JR's Bar & Grill (4, C7)

The busiest gay bar in Dupont Circle, if not the busiest gay bar in DC, brings to mind Armistead Maupin's acronym 'NACAM' (not as cute as me) – tons of men, tons of noise and tons of attitude.

✉ 1519 17th St NW
☎ 328-0090
Ⓜ Dupont Circle
🚌 G2 ⏱ noon-2am (Fri-Sat to 3am)
💲 free

Voices of the Community

For a fun alternative to the bars, check out the award-winning **Gay Men's Chorus of Washington, DC** (GMCW; ☎ 338-7464, @ www.gmcw.org). The chorus performs three seasonal concerts per year and appears at a variety of community events taking place at venues all over the city. Their mission statement lists the group's objectives as follows: 'To develop a musical legacy, to affirm the role of the gay community in the life of the nation and humanity, to educate others about the gay experience, and to inspire through music.' The chorus has received rave reviews from the *Washington Post* and other publications, and has released a number of full-length albums. You can call or visit the GMCW website for schedule and ticket information.
– *David Zingarelli & Vivek Waglé*

Lizard Lounge (4, C7)
The place of the moment for dancing on Sunday, this upscale club pounds with techno sounds that draw a mainly young, mainly white, mainly male, totally hip crowd.
✉ 1520 14th St NW ☎ 331-4422 ℮ www.atlasevents.com 🚍 52, 53, 54, G2 ⏲ Sun 8pm-2am ⑤ free

Omega DC (5, A3)
The busiest bar on the strip west of the Circle is hidden in an alley near the corner of 22nd and P Sts. Choose between the conventional bar downstairs and a video bar upstairs (music videos in the bar, porn videos in the adjoining room; look but don't touch).
✉ 2122 P St NW ☎ 223-4917 Ⓜ Dupont Circle 🚍 G2 ⏲ 4pm-2am (Fri-Sat to 3am) ⑤ free

More Gay & Lesbian Washington
Detailed information for gay and lesbian visitors to Washington can be found on pages 118 to 119. The following businesses cater to a gay and lesbian clientele or tend to draw lots of gay and lesbian patrons:

Carlyle Suites Hotel (p. 104) – a place to stay

18th & U Duplex Diner (2004 18th St NW; ☎ 265-7828) – a place to eat or drink

Lambda Rising (p. 62) – a place for books

The Nation (p. 95) – the place to dance on Saturday night

Results the Gym (p. 46) – a place to work out

Phase 1 (5, G11)
One of the hot women's spots in town includes a tiny dance floor, a regulation pool table and a big-screen TV (for the football games).
✉ 525 8th St SE ☎ 544-6831 Ⓜ Eastern Market ⏲ Sun & Thurs 7pm-2am, Fri-Sat 7pm-3am ⑤ $5 Fri-Sat

Remington's (4, F11)
At this country-western bar and dance hall, you can learn the two-step Monday and Thursday 8:30-9:30pm or Fridays 8-8:45pm (no extra charge).
✉ 639 Pennsylvania Ave SE ☎ 543-3113 Ⓜ Eastern Market ⏲ 4pm-2am (Fri-Sat to 3am) ⑤ free

Checking out the scene at the Lizard Lounge

Rick Gerharter

SPECTATOR SPORTS

Washington lost its major league baseball team years ago, which gives locals an excuse to visit the Orioles at Camden Yards in Baltimore. Otherwise, you'll find all the spectator sport options you'd expect in a large North American city.

Tickets to most professional sports events are handled by **TicketMaster** (☎ 432-7328, 800-551-7328). If you can't get a ticket directly, try the concierge of your hotel or look at the classified ads in the *Post.*

Football

The **Washington Redskins** are not just a football team; they're a passion that unites all Greater Washington. When the 'Skins are playing, the city retreats to its sports bars and living rooms to cheer on the team. The 'Skins play all the way out at **FedEx Field** (1600 Raljon Rd, Landover, MD; 🚗 Central Ave exit on I-495). Don't even think about going there unless you're willing to buy a ticket from a scalper: the game will be totally sold out before you arrive. The **Baltimore Ravens**, another NFL franchise, play in PSINet Stadium at Baltimore's Camden Yards (see Baseball).

Baseball

The **Baltimore Orioles** take the field in downtown Baltimore, about an hour's ride from Union Station on MARC or Amtrak trains, or a slightly longer trip if you take the $9 bus ride from the Greenbelt Metro station. Oriole Park at **Camden Yards** (333 Camden St, Baltimore, MD; 1, B4; ☎ 410-481-7328; 🚗 I-95 north to Camden Yards exit) is the model for the new baseball-only parks springing up across North America, combining the best features of classic old parks like Wrigley Field and Fenway with modern conveniences like unimpaired sightlines.

Basketball

Michael Jordan bought a piece of the **Washington Wizards** a couple of years ago and came out of retirement in the fall of 2001 to try to lead the

team to his heights of glory. Whether he'll do so remains to be seen as of press time, but as long as he's playing or working the sidelines, NBA games in DC will be interesting. The team plays at the **MCI Center** (601 F St NW; 5, D10; ☎ 628-3200; Ⓜ Gallery Pl/Chinatown).

If you prefer consistent winners or you just like college basketball, the often successful **Georgetown Hoyas** promise a good ride. They also play at the MCI Center. Tickets are cheaper, though not necessarily easier to come by – particularly if the team is headed to the NCAA Final Four.

Ice Hockey

Every city in North America has an NHL franchise, it seems, whether the city ices over in the winter or not. Washington's no exception. The **Washington Capitals** play at the MCI Center. Come cheer them on, or come cheer established opponents like the Maple Leafs or the Bruins.

Horse Racing

The English gentry and would-be gentry who settled this part of the world loved horses and horse racing, and the tradition survives around Greater Washington. The **Pimlico Race Course** in Baltimore (Winner & Hayward Aves; 1, B4; ☎ 410-542-9400; e www.pimlinco.com) hosts the Preakness the third Saturday of May and other races from April to June and from July to September. **Laurel Park**, halfway to Baltimore (Racetrack Rd off Route 198, Laurel, MD; 1, B4; ☎ 301-725-0400) offers racing throughout the year. The **Rosecroft Raceway** (6336 Rosecroft Dr, Fort Washington, MD; ☎ 301-567-4000; e www.rosecroft.com) features harness racing year round.

Bill Bachman

Camden Yards was instrumental in ushering in the new era of non-ugly baseball parks.

places to stay

Nearly 20 million people visit Washington every year, and most need somewhere to stay. At last count there were more than 100 hotels in the District of Columbia with over 24,000 hotel rooms (not including the rows of chain hotels and such lining the Virginia shore from Rosslyn to Arlington to Alexandria).

Most of these hotels were built and geared for modern business travelers. Some, though, were designed for businesspeople of an earlier age, when legislators and lobbyists lived in hotels while Congress was in session. Still others were built as houses or apartment buildings and converted to hotels in later lives.

Room Rates

The price ranges in this chapter indicate the cost of a standard double room before the 14.5% DC hotel tax.

Top End	from $200
Mid-Range	$125-199
Budget	under $125

Rick Gerharter

You'll find hotels almost everywhere in visitor's Washington, from Capitol Hill to Downtown and Georgetown, and up the Connecticut Ave corridor from Downtown to Dupont Circle and Woodley Park.

The cost of a room varies wildly depending on the market and season. Prices are usually highest in spring and fall, when the weather is nice, Congress is in session and the convention business is roaring. Rates fall off on weekends, in July and August and again in January and February. Recent reports show average room rates in the city hovering between $125 and $135, slightly higher than in Chicago but lot lower than in New York. The events of September 11, 2001, put a crimp in business travel, so rates in 2002 and beyond could be reduced significantly, particularly if you shop around.

Soak up the luxurious atmosphere at Washington's fine hotels.

Rick Gerharter

TOP END

Four Seasons (2, D4)
Before there were Four Seasons hotels everywhere from Boston to Beverly Hills, this one was attracting the wealthy and the expense-account crowds with its vibrant lobby, luxurious three-level spa overlooking the C&O Canal, quiet guest rooms and sensational service.
✉ **2800 Pennsylvania Ave NW** ☎ 342-0444, 800-332-3442; fax 344-1673 e www.four seasons.com Ⓜ Foggy Bottom/GWU 🚌 30, 32, 34, 35, 36, Georgetown Shuttles ✕ Seasons

George Washington University Inn (5, D1)
A 1980s apartment building nicely converted into an all-suites hotel, this place is convenient to the Kennedy Center and GWU, as well as the Foggy Bottom/GWU Metro. Every room has a microwave, a fridge and a coffeemaker, so you can settle in for an extended stay.
✉ **824 New Hampshire Ave NW** ☎ 337-6620, 800-426-4455; fax 298-7499 e www .gwuinn.com Ⓜ Foggy Bottom/GWU ✕ Foggy Bottom Café at 924 25th St NW

Georgetown Inn
(2, C2) The Georgetown Inn provides a marginally less expensive alternative to the Four Seasons for visitors who want to be in the heart of Georgetown. The 96 rooms feature traditional furnishings such as four-poster beds and

Bookings
The Washington, DC, Convention & Tourism Corporation maintains a hotel booking service on its website (e www.washington.org); alternatively, call them at ☎ 800-847-4832. BNBInns.com represents approximately 25 small hotels and B&Bs at e www.bnbinns.com/states/DC.htm.

modern amenities such as marble baths, double-paned windows (for street noise) and high-speed Internet access.
✉ **1310 Wisconsin Ave NW** ☎ 333-8900; fax 333-8308 e www .georgetowninn.com Ⓜ Foggy Bottom/GWU 🚌 30, 32, 34, 35, 36, Georgetown Shuttles ✕ Daily Grill (p. 79)

Hotel George (5, E13)
Eurosleek style – no chintz, no club chairs– provides the atmosphere in this renovated building around the corner from Union Station. The food matches this style at Bis, a new venture from the chef at Vidalia. It's very popular with New Yorkers, not merely because it's so close to the station.
✉ **15 E St NW** ☎ 347-4200, 800-576-8331; fax 347-4213 e www.hotelgeorge .com Ⓜ Union Station ✕ Bis

Hotel Washington (5, E6) The other historic hotel in the capital (besides the Willard), next door to its illustrious counterpart and across the street from the Treasury Building, offers large rooms with

appropriately traditional appointments, as well as the best view in town from the top-floor restaurant and Sky Terrace.
✉ **15th St & Pennsylvania Ave NW** ☎ 638-5900, 800-241-3848; fax 638-1595 e www.hotel washington.com Ⓜ Metro Center, McPherson Square ✕ Two Continents Restaurant

Rick Gerharter

The Willard's archrival

Valets at the Jefferson are highly trained parallel parkers.

Rick Gerharter

Jefferson Hotel (5, B5)

Originally a splendid early-20th-century apartment building, the Jefferson was converted into a 100-room hotel for Washington movers and shakers by the late Edward Bennett Williams. This is where presidential advisor Dick Morris spent his afternoons brushing up on his podiatry with a call girl. It's very quiet, very elegant and very expensive.

✉ 1200 16th St NW ☎ 347-2200, 800-235-6397; fax 331-7982 🄴 www.loewshotels .com Ⓜ Farragut North ✗ Jefferson's

Marriott Wardman Park (4, A5)

The largest single hotel in the city, this Marriott boasts over 1300 rooms and more than 95,000 sq ft of exhibit space, which should say it all. Ask for a room in the charming original Wardman wing.

✉ 2660 Woodley Rd NW ☎ 328-2000, 800-228-9290; fax 234-0015 🄴 www.marriott.com Ⓜ Woodley Park/Zoo ✗ Perle's

The Mayflower (5, B5)

This is the kind of place Judy Holiday stayed in the movie *Born Yesterday* – a grand hotel of the old school. The block-long lobby is lit with chandeliers, the marble floors shine, the staff glides about like palace retainers. Not even the TVs in the bathrooms can disturb the picture of pre-WWII elegance.

✉ 1127 Connecticut Ave NW ☎ 347-3000, 800-228-7697; fax 466-9083 🄴 www .renaissancehotels.com Ⓜ Farragut North ✗ Café Promenade

Morrison-Clark Historic Inn & Restaurant (5, B8)

It's a toss-up which is better – the Morrison-Clark's rooms or its food. The rooms are stunning – 19th-century furnishings with 21st-century amenities, from dryers to data ports. The restaurant is a knockout, with modern American food (Southern-style) in some of the prettiest dining rooms in town.

✉ 11th St & Massachusetts Ave NW ☎ 898-7898; fax 289-8576 🄴 www.morrison clark.com 🚇 G8 ✗ Morrison-Clark Restaurant

Park Hyatt (5, B2)

When is a Hyatt not a Hyatt? When it's the Park Hyatt in Washington, where the guest rooms are as luxurious as the lobbies. With TVs in the armoires and the bathrooms, and large living areas, you'd think you were in a grand European hotel.

✉ 24th & M Sts NW ☎ 789-1234, 800-233-1234; fax 457-8823 🄴 www.hyatt.com Ⓜ Foggy Bottom/GWU ✗ Melrose

---

The Usual Suspects

All the big US hotel chains have properties in Washington or across the river in Arlington. In addition to the chain hotels listed in this chapter, you can find four **Holiday Inns** (☎ 800-445-8667), three **Hiltons** (☎ 800-445-8667), two more **Hyatts** (☎ 800-233-1234), two **Westins** (☎ 800-228-3000), two **Wyndhams** (☎ 800-996-3426) and a half-dozen **Marriotts** (☎ 800-228-9290).

Phoenix Park Hotel

(5, E13) Of the Irish, by the Irish, for everyone, the Phoenix Park is a business traveler's hotel with the feel of a rural house in the old country. Across the street from Union Station and two blocks from the Capitol, it's also home of The Dubliner, the best Irish bar in town.

✉ 520 N Capitol St NW ☎ 638-6900; fax 393-3236 e www .phoenixparkhotel.com Ⓜ Union Station ✕ The Dubliner (p. 94)

St Gregory Hotel & Suites (5, B3)

Owned by the same family that owns and operates the Governor's House, the St Gregory is a little flashier and a little pricier, appropriate for the location where Downtown hits the West End. Half of the 154 rooms have full kitchens; all of them have big bathrooms, CD players and Web TV.

✉ 2033 M St NW ☎ 530-3600, 800-829-5034; fax 466-7353

e www.capital1hotel swdc.com Ⓜ Dupont Circle, Farragut North ✕ Donna's Café & Coffee Bar

Swissôtel (4, D5)

The Swissôtel features rooms with views, sprawling up and down and across the Potomac from the Watergate complex (yes, that Watergate). Room interiors are spacious and elegant in a European-living-room kind of way, with marble tubs in the baths, in-room fax machines and other gadgets for guests.

✉ 2650 Virginia Ave NW ☎ 965-2300, 800-424-2736; fax 337-7915 e www.swissotel.com Ⓜ Foggy Botttom/GWU ✕ Jeffrey's

Washington Court Hotel (5, E12)

A business and convention hotel well located near Union Station, the Washington Court has recently been refurbished to freshen all the guest rooms and public spaces. The south side of the

upper floors features great Capitol views. This is a good place for bargain hunting on weekends or when Congress is out of town.

✉ 525 New Jersey Ave NW ☎ 628-2100, 800-321-3010; fax 879-7918 e www.washington courthotel.com Ⓜ Union Station ✕ Café & Grill Restaurant

Willard Intercontinental

(5, E7) The Willard is the most important hotel in Washington history; every president has stayed here since 1853. US Grant spent so much time in the hotel that influence peddlers took up residence in the lobby, earning the moniker 'lobbyists.' Polished and refurbished from top to bottom, it sparkles as it did back in Grant's day.

✉ 1401 Pennsylvania Ave NW ☎ 628-9100, 800-327-0200; fax 637-7326 e www.six continentshotels.com Ⓜ Metro Center ✕ The Willard Room

During Christmastime, the Mayflower's lobby is reminiscent of a cathedral.

Rick Gerharter

MID-RANGE

Kitchen Privileges

If you're headed to Washington for an extended period, you'll want to consider a place where you can fix your own breakfast or reheat a takeaway meal. The **Hotel Lombardy** (below), **Lincoln Suites** (p. 105) and **Carlyle Suites** (below) are our favorite choices in the town center. Other options include two **Marriott Residence Inns** (☎ 800-228-9290) and the **Remington Executive Suites** in Foggy Bottom (601 24th St NW; ☎ 223-4512, 800-225-3847; **e** www.remington-dc.com).

Capitol Hill Suites

(5, H14) Clean, basic suites with kitchens or kitchenettes are the order of the day at this spot, a few steps from the Capitol South Metro station and a few blocks from the Capitol itself. It's popular with intern types, but you don't have to be under 30 to check in or fit in.

⊠ 200 C St SE ☎ 543-6000; fax 547-2608 **Ⓜ** Capitol South **✕** Le Bon Café (p. 77)

Carlyle Suites Hotel

(4, C7) The only art deco hotel in town, the Carlyle sports a pink-and-black color scheme you won't see repeated many places. The rooms are large and well equipped, if a little tired. The location, near the Dupont Circle Metro, the 17th St bars, the New U and Adams-Morgan, is very lively.

⊠ 1731 New Hampshire Ave NW ☎ 234-3200; fax 387-0085 **Ⓜ** Dupont Circle **✕** Randolph's Grill

Channel Inn Hotel

(4, G8) Slightly schizophrenic, the Channel Inn features an outside that looks like a motel and an inside that looks like a comfortable English country inn – and then there are those views of the monuments and the Washington Channel. It's popular with tour groups (if you've got your own bus, the waterfront location is no problem).

⊠ 650 Water St SW ☎ 554-2400, 800-368-5668; fax 863-1164 **Ⓜ** Waterfront **✕** Pier 7

Governor's House Hotel

(5, A5) A newish hotel owned and operated by a local family, the Governor's House is blocks from the White House, close to the lawyers and lobbyists on K, L and M Sts. Amenities include Web TV and passes to the fancy YMCA around the corner.

⊠ 1615 Rhode Island Ave NW ☎ 296-2100, 800-821-4367; fax 331-0227 **e** www.capital hotelswdc.com **Ⓜ** Farragut North **✕** 17th St Bar & Grill

Hotel Lombardy

(5, C3) If you have to move into a hotel for a month, this is the one. Built as an apartment building in the 1920s, it retains the charm of that time without sacrificing the conveniences of this time. With elegant rooms featuring fresh flowers and crisp linens, who could ask for more?

⊠ 2019 Pennsylvania Ave NW ☎ 828-2600, 800-424-5486; fax 872-0503 **e** www.hotel lombardy.com **Ⓜ** Foggy Bottom/GWU, Farragut West **✕** Venetian Room

Hotel Monticello

(2, D4) Forty-seven charming little suites, furnished and fitted with conveniences just as Jefferson would have wished, lie on a side street right off the M St hubbub. Expect some traffic noise in the rooms facing the street. There's limited parking for small to mid-sized cars, so call ahead if driving is part of your plan.

⊠ 1075 Thomas Jefferson St NW ☎ 337-0900; fax 333-6526 **Ⓜ** Foggy Bottom/GWU 🚌 30, 32, 34, 35, 36, Georgetown Shuttles **✕** Bistro Français (p. 83)

Jury's Normandy Hotel

(4, B6) Run by the same nice folks who run the Jury's on Dupont Circle and the Courtyard Inn next door, the Normandy has lovely guest rooms, a nice breakfast parlor and a good location uphill from the Dupont Circle Metro.

⊠ 2118 Wyoming Ave ☎ 483-1350, 800-423-6953; fax 387-8241 **e** www.jurysdoyle.com **Ⓜ** Dupont Circle **✕** Afterwords Café

Jury's Washington Hotel (4, C6)

At the top end of the mid-range, this may be the best value in Washington. First, there's the location, right on Dupont Circle. Then there are the guest rooms, elegant without being fussy, with all the amenities. Finally, there's the friendly, competent Irish-accented service.

✉ **1500 New Hampshire Ave NW ☎ 483-6000, 800-423-6953; fax 328-3265 e www.jurys doyle.com Ⓜ Dupont Circle ✕ Claddagh's Restaurant**

Lincoln Suites (5, B4)

One of the best values for an all-suites hotel, the Lincoln lies in the snappy part of Downtown west of Connecticut Ave. It's a rela-tively small (99-room) prop-erty offering newspapers and continental breakfast in the morning, good areas for working in the evening, and cookies and milk for a snack at bedtime.

✉ **1823 L St NW ☎ 223-4320; fax 223-8546 e www.lincoln hotels.com Ⓜ Farragut North ✕ Luigi's at 19th & L Sts NW**

Swann House (4, C7)

This B&B in a historic brick mansion is consistently rated the best in the District. Private baths in each room and the small swimming pool in the back set it miles apart from the competition. It's convenient to Dupont Circle, the 17th St strip, the New U and Adams-Morgan.

✉ **1808 New Hamp-shire Ave ☎ 265-4414; fax 265-6755 e stay@ swannhouse.com Ⓜ Dupont Circle ✕ Café Luna at 1633 P St NW**

BUDGET

Adams Inn (3, B2)

The Adams comprises two adjacent row houses on a residential street two blocks from the center of Adams-Morgan. Rooms are simple, clean and well maintained. The parlors are comfortable places to lounge during the day. There's no smoking indoors, but you'll find plenty of room on the exte-rior porches.

✉ **1744 Lanier Pl NW ☎ 745-3600, 800-578-6807; fax 319-7958 e www.adamsinn.com Ⓜ Woodley Park/Zoo 🚌 42 ✕ The Diner (p. 73)**

Allen Lee Hotel (5, E2)

The 79 rooms at the Allen Lee, most without bath-rooms, are housed in a building near GWU that will remind you of an old college dormitory, the one that was vacuumed the first of the month whether it needed it or not. If you're traveling on a very tight budget this may just be the right spot for you.

✉ **2224 F St NW ☎ 331-1224, 800-4621-0186; fax 296-3158 e www.allenlee hotel.com Ⓜ Foggy Bottom/GWU ✕ The Watergate**

Brickskeller Inn (4, C6)

Of the forty guest rooms of the Brickskeller Inn, only two boast private baths. All rooms are nes-tled upstairs from the saloon famous for the world's largest selection of beers. The convenient and lively Dupont Circle loca-tion and extremely low prices compensate for a certain lack of charm about the place.

✉ **1523 22nd St NW ☎ 293-1885 fax 293-0996 Ⓜ Dupont Circle ✕ SoHo Tea at 22nd & P Sts NW**

Rick Gerharter

Roving with Rover

As the number of cats and dogs in the US surpasses the number of children, lots of properties welcome your four-legged companions, particularly dogs that weigh less than 25lbs (or so) and cats that have been declawed. Pet-friendly spots range from the tony **Jefferson Hotel** (p. 102) and **Swann House** (above) to the chains, including the **Hilton** (p. 102), the **Marriotts** (p. 104) and the **Days Inn** (p. 106). Call ahead to confirm details on their policies.

Embassy Inn (4, C7)

A European-style hotel on a pleasant tree-lined block, the Embassy Inn is on the east side of the Dupont Circle neighborhood. Small rooms come with basic amenities, continental breakfast and afternoon snacks.

✉ 1627 16th St NW
☎ 234-7800, 800-423-9111; fax 667-4503
Ⓜ Dupont Circle
🚌 S1, S2, S3
✕ Café Luna at 1633 P St NW

Hotel Harrington

(5, E8) This family-run property has been catering to tourists on a budget for a couple of generations. The rooms are small and unappealing, but the location is good and the prices are great.

✉ 11th & E Sts NW
☎ 628-8140, 800-424-8532; fax 347-3924
🅴 www.hotel-harrington.com
Ⓜ Federal Triangle, Metro Center ✕ Harry's

India House DC

(6, D6) At the border of the 'People's Republic' of Takoma Park, Maryland, sits one of the three hostels in the Greater Washington area. Only steps from the Takoma Metro station and 20 minutes from the city center, it's clean, features friendly managers and sports a big backyard to hang out in during those deliciously warm summer nights.

✉ 300 Carroll St NW
☎ 291-1195 Ⓜ Takoma
✕ Taliano's at Carroll & Maple Sts NW

Tabard Inn (5, A5)

This genteel country inn, just off Dupont Circle, offers travelers an idiosyncratic selection of guest rooms (some with private bathrooms), each with Green Acres–style decoration. The restaurant and gardens on the grounds are worth a stopover even if you plan on sleeping elsewhere.

✉ 1739 N St NW
☎ 785-1277; fax 785-6173 🅴 www.tabardinn.com Ⓜ Dupont Circle ✕ Tabard Inn Restaurant

Washington International Student Center (3, C2)

The Adams-Morgan counterpart to the Washington International Youth hostel, this spot provides no-frills dorm housing in a five-bedroom building right on the neighborhood's main drag. Internet access and a lack of curfew are additional draws for students and other traveling types on the backpacking circuit.

✉ 2451 18th St NW

☎ 667-7681, 800-567-4150 Ⓜ Woodley Park/Zoo 🚌 90, 92, 93, 94, 96, 98, L2, U-Link ✕ The Diner (p. 73)

Takin' off from the Tabard

Washington International Youth Hostel (5, C8)

The only hostel downtown boasts 250 beds in single-sex dorm rooms and in family rooms. With no lock-out time, it's a good base for exploring DC's nightlife.

✉ 1009 11th St NW
☎ 737-2333, 800-909-4776; fax 731-1508
Ⓜ Metro Center 🚌 66, G8 ✕ Haad Thai at 1100 New York Ave NW

Windsor Park (4, B6)

This quiet, 43-room property is a little large for a B&B, a little small for a hotel. This allows it to offer the amenities of a hotel along with the traditional breakfasts and papers of B&Bs.

✉ 2116 Kalorama Rd NW ☎ 483-7700, 800-247-3064; fax 332-4547
🅴 www.windsorparkhotel.com Ⓜ Dupont Circle, Woodley Park/Zoo 🚌 L1, L4 ✕ Woodley Inn

Motels

If you're on a budget, driving to town and don't mind being tied to your auto while you're sightseeing, the strip of motels on New York Ave NE (US Rte 50 to you) may be just what you're looking for. Choices include the **Super 8 Motel** (501 New York Ave NE, ☎ 543-7400), **HoJo Inn** (600 New York Ave NE, ☎ 546-9200) and **Days Inn** (2700 New York Ave NE, ☎ 832-5800).

facts for the visitor

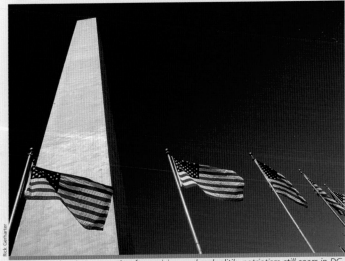

Rick Gerharter

Despite the city's reputation for cynicism and realpolitik, patriotism still soars in DC.

ARRIVAL & DEPARTURE

Washington lies at the southern end of the busy Boston-Washington air shuttle corridor and is a major hub for east-west flights in North America. Since September 11, 2001, increased security checks and restrictions on flights into Reagan National Airport have substantially slashed the shuttle business, forcing legions of New Yorkers onto the trains.

Baltimore-Washington International and Dulles International Airports continue to serve nonstop flights to most major cities in the US and Canada, nonstop flights to major European destinations and at least one daily nonstop flight to Tokyo. Travelers from elsewhere in Asia or Europe can make connections in New York, London, Paris, Frankfurt or Amsterdam. Travelers from East Asia or the South Pacific can make connections in West Coast cities such as Los Angeles or San Francisco.

Air

Three major airports serve the capital. All are well connected to the city by rapid transit facilities, commuter rail or conventional ground transportation.

Reagan National Airport

National Airport (4, K7), renamed for 'The Gipper' a few years back, is so close to town you'd think it was a train terminal. With millions of passengers running through the place each year, it can feel like one, too. It handles short and medium-length runs, such as the shuttles to New York and Boston, from two new terminal buildings (B and C). The events of September 11, 2001, resulted in some service cutbacks; check for details.

Left Luggage
Storage lockers have been removed for the indefinite future.

Information
General Inquiries
☎ 703-417-8000

Flight Information

America West	☎	800-235-9292
American	☎	800-223-5436
Continental	☎	800-525-0280
Delta	☎	800-221-1212
Northwest	☎	800-225-2525
United	☎	800-241-6522
US Airways	☎	800-428-4322

Parking Information
☎ 703-417-4311

Hotel Booking Service
There is no booking service at National Airport, but the airport authority does maintain a list of area lodgings at their website (e www.metwashairports.com/national/hotels.htm).

Airport Access
Metrorail's Blue Line and Yellow Line stop at the station opposite Terminals B and C. Trains run Monday to Thursday 5:30am- or 6am-midnight, Friday and Saturday 5:30am- or 6am-2am, Sunday 8am-midnight. One-way fares to downtown Washington are under $2. Travel time to downtown is about 20 minutes; add 10 minutes or so if you have to transfer to another Metro line.

SuperShuttle vans go to downtown hotels for $9 per person. Flag down a blue van on the curb outside baggage claim. To book a pickup for a trip to the airport, call ☎ 800-258-3826.

Find taxis at the stands in front of each terminal. Fares to downtown run about $12-15. Some drivers charge a $1 surcharge for trips from National.

Dulles International Airport

Dulles (1, B3), about 28 miles west of town on the edge of Virginia hunt country, serves long-haul and international flights. An East Coast hub for United Airlines, it currently handles over 19 million passengers a year and long ago outgrew its signature terminal building by Eero Saarinen. Travelers passing through Dulles should expect long drives from the city, long lines for the mobile lounges that carry people from the old terminal building to the new terminal across the tarmac, and long hikes in the new terminal building. Allow plenty of time.

Left Luggage

Storage lockers have been removed for the indefinite future.

Information

General Inquiries
☎ 703-572-2700

Flight Information
See Information under Reagan National Airport.

Parking Information
☎ 703-572-4500

Hotel Booking Service
The Hotel Phone Center on the lower level of the Main Terminal offers complimentary telephone connections to several nearby hotels.

Airport Access

The Washington Flyer company runs a shuttle every half-hour (on the quarter- and three-quarter-hour) to the West Falls Church Metro station (6, F1). The trip takes about 30 minutes and costs $8/14 one-way/roundtrip. Get tickets either on the lower level of the Main Terminal (inbound) or at the West Falls Church Metro station (outbound).

Washington Flyer also operates taxis from the taxi stands in front of the Main Terminal. Fares to downtown hotels run between $40 and $50 without tip.

Baltimore-Washington International Airport

BWI (1, B4) is the stepsister of the DC airports, about 30 miles northeast of downtown, but it has enjoyed new-found popularity since Southwest and other low-cost or short-haul airlines started service. You can catch a handful of coast-to-coast and international flights here as well; check website (**e** www .bwiairport.com) for details.

Left Luggage

BWI no longer offers storage lockers.

Information

General Inquiries
☎ 800-435-9294

Flight Information
Southwest ☎ 800-435-9792
For other numbers, see Information under Reagan National Airport.

Parking Information
☎ 800-468-6294

Hotel Booking Service
BWI does not have a hotel booking service, but the BWI website offers a list of nearby hotels and motels.

Airport Access

Amtrak and the Maryland State commuter rail system (MARC) run trains between Union Station and a BWI stop, with free shuttle buses for the 10-minute ride to the BWI terminal. Amtrak tickets cost more ($20 and up each way versus $5 and up for MARC), but Amtrak trains are five to 10 minutes faster and Amtrak is the only way to get there on the weekends. Avoid the ticket lines at Union Station by buying a roundtrip ticket at BWI.

SuperShuttle offers van service from BWI to DC, Maryland suburbs, and northern Virginia. Fares average $26 to $32 (additional passengers $8). Express service (no sharing) is available; call ☎ 800-258-3826 for details and for return service (24hr advance notice required).

Taxis are available on the lower level. Fares to downtown DC run about $55 without tip.

Bus

Washington is a hub for bus travel. Greyhound (☎ 298-5154, 800-231-2222; e www.greyhound.com) provides nationwide service from its main station, downtown at 1005 1st St NE (4, D10), behind Union Station, and limited service from Union Station itself.

Train

Washington has some of the best rail service in the US, with direct Amtrak service (☎ 800-872-7245; e www.amtrak.com) from Union Station north to New York and Boston, south to Florida and west to Chicago and the rest of the country. The Metroliner and Acela Express lines to New York go head-to-head with the airlines – perhaps the only route in the US where rail competes directly with air.

Travel Documents

Passport
Canadians need proof of Canadian citizenship or a passport to enter the US. All other visitors must have a valid passport, which should be valid for at least six months longer than their intended stay in the US.

Visa
If you're from Argentina, Australia, Austria, Belgium, Denmark, France, Germany, Ireland, Italy, Japan, the Netherlands, New Zealand, Spain, Switzerland or the UK, you can enter the US for up to 90 days without a visa provided you have a roundtrip ticket that's nonrefundable in the US, plus a passport valid for at least six months past your scheduled departure date. For an updated list of countries included in the visa waiver program, see the Immigration and Naturalization Service's website (e www.ins.gov) or call ☎ 800-375-5283. All other travelers need a visitor's visa, which can be obtained at most US consulate offices overseas; it's generally easier to obtain a visa from an office in one's home country.

Return/Onward Ticket
Travelers under the reciprocal visa waiver program need return or onward tickets to enter the US. Travelers applying for visas overseas often must present such tickets as proof of their intent to return home.

Customs

All incoming travelers must fill out customs declarations, disclosing all agricultural products and all cash and cash equivalents worth $10,000 or more in their possession.

Duty Free

Overseas visitors may bring in up to $100 in goods or gifts duty-free, together with 100 cigars, 200 cigarettes and a liter of alcoholic beverages. As of this writing, Cuban tobacco products are still prohibited in the US.

Departure Tax

There are no separate departure taxes to leave a US airport. Any airport charges are included in the cost of your ticket.

GETTING AROUND

Driving in the District is usually a fool's errand. The traffic comes at you from all directions down the boulevards and through the traffic circles. On-street parking is impossible during peak hours and tough the rest of the time. Most visitor sites are within a few blocks of the Metro, except Georgetown and Adams-Morgan, which are good 10-minute hikes from the nearest stations.

The entire city is laid out in a grid radiating from the Capitol, with diagonal avenues crisscrossing the whole mess. The center of the city is easy to navigate. North-south streets are numbered and east-west streets are lettered, so the corner of 7th & F Sts NW is seven blocks west and five blocks north of the Capitol. (7th & F St SW is seven blocks west and five blocks south). There are no B, J, X, Y or Z Sts.

Travel Passes

The Metrorail system sells daily passes ($5), good from 9:30am weekdays and all day on weekends, or weekly passes ($17.50), good anytime. The $30 weekly pass covers travel on both the Metro and Metrobus. You can buy passes at most Metro stations, at the Metro Center station (12th & G Sts; 5, D8), at some Safeway and Giant supermarkets, and online at their website (e www.wmata.com).

Subway

The Metrorail (☎ 637-7000) subway and elevated lines serve almost every part of the District, except Georgetown and Adams-Morgan, and huge stretches of the suburbs on either side of the Potomac River. Large, comfortable, clean trains run frequently from about 5:30am to about midnight daily. Stations are clean and safe, if a little austere. Fares start at $1.10 and vary depending on the length of the journey and the time of day. You pay the fare with a pass (see above section) or a fare card, purchased at any station machine. Metro's website (e www .wmata.com) has timetables.

In this book, the nearest Metro station is noted after the Ⓜ icon in each listing.

Bus

Metrobuses serve the entire city, including Georgetown and Adams-Morgan, and most of the inner suburbs. Most buses run until midnight. Check timetables at Metro stations or online at e www.wmata.com, or pick up a route map ($1.50) at Metro Center (12th & G Sts; 5, D8). Fares in DC are $1.10 standard, $2 for express buses or 25¢ with a Metrorail transfer (pick it up at the station before you board the train). Transfers from regular Metrobus lines to any other regular lines are free. On some lines, drivers will drop you almost anywhere you want after 9pm to save you having to walk from designated stops.

Metro now runs shuttles to Georgetown from the Dupont Circle, Foggy Bottom/GWU and Rosslyn Metro stations; service starts at 9:45am and stops at midnight Sunday to Thursday and 2am Friday and Saturday. The fare is 50¢ (25¢ with a Metrorail transfer). Metro also runs the U-Link shuttle to Adams-Morgan from the Woodley Park/Zoo and U St/Cardozo Metro stations. Regular fares apply.

In this book, the nearest bus line is noted after the 🚌 icon in the listings.

Train

The Maryland Rail Commuter System (MARC; ☎ 800-325-7245; e www.mtamaryland.com) serves Baltimore, the Maryland suburbs and the eastern edge of West Virginia with three rail lines running from Union Station (5, E14). MARC trains operate on weekdays only, approximately 5am-midnight. Fares vary depending on the length of the trip; a one-way fare from DC to Baltimore costs about $6.

The Virginia Rain Express (VRE; ☎ 800-743-3873; e www.vre.org) serves the Virginia suburbs with a line to Manassas and another line to Fredericksburg. VRE trains stop at Union Station and at the L'Enfant Plaza Metro in Southwest DC. Fares vary depending on the length of the trip; a one-way fare from Union Station to Fredericksburg will cost about $7.

Taxi

Taxis are easy to come by in the center of the city and the busier areas of the Northwest quadrant. You can hail a taxi on the street, line up at taxi stands in front of large hotels and shopping complexes, or call for a cab from one of the major companies, such as Capitol (☎ 546-2400), Diamond (☎ 387-6200) or Yellow (☎ 544-1212).

The city that gave us the Internal Revenue Code has also applied its genius for byzantine rate structures to the taxi-fare system. Don't expect taxi meters. Instead, taxis charge by zone – there's a basic charge of $4 to travel within one zone (eg, Capitol Hill to Dupont Circle) and an additional charge of $1.50 for each extra zone. You'll pay a $1 surcharge at peak hours and other surcharges for different kinds of baggage. Drivers can pick up two more passengers (their choice, not yours) if the new passengers don't take everyone more than five blocks out of the way. Therefore, hail any cab that goes by even if it's partly occupied.

Car & Motorcycle

Driving in Washington is difficult but not impossible. If you need a car, your biggest problems will be making your way through the traffic circles and finding parking, which is usually available but often expensive. Expect a challenge parking in Georgetown or Adams-Morgan on a Saturday night, and don't even think about parking on the street downtown during peak hours. There are no large garages operated by the city. You can find privately operated parking garages under the Washington Hilton (1919 Connecticut Ave; 4, B6), where rates are $5/hr, $15/day, and under the Georgetown Park Mall (M St & Wisconsin Ave; 2, D2), which charges $4/hr. Smaller lots are scattered around the north end of downtown and the fringes of Adams-Morgan and Georgetown.

Road Rules

As drivers do throughout the USA, Washingtonians drive on the right side of the road. You are permitted to turn right on a red light after a full stop unless the intersection is marked with a sign to the contrary. Look before you turn, because such signs sometimes appear at every other intersection. All front-seat passengers must wear seatbelts. Children under three must be strapped into safety seats.

The basic speed limit is 25mph on city streets and 55mph on highways (sometimes 65mph). Driving under the influence of alcohol or drugs is strictly prohibited. Be very careful to avoid it: you don't want to see the inside of the DC criminal justice system.

Rental

If you do need a car, you can rent one from any of the large national car rental chains, such as Alamo (☎ 800-462-5266), Avis (☎ 800-230-4898), Budget (☎ 800-527-0700), Hertz (☎ 800-654-3131), National (☎ 800-227-7368) or Thrifty (☎ 800-847-4389). You'll need a valid driver's license and a recognized credit card. Keep in mind that no one rents to drivers under 21, and many companies refuse to rent to drivers under 25.

Driver's License & Permit

Canadian and Mexican driving licenses are generally accepted in the DC area. Other overseas travelers should carry their domestic driving licenses and an international driving permit.

Motoring Organizations

The American Automobile Association (AAA; ☎ 800-922-8228; e www.aaa.com), the preeminent motoring organization in the US, provides minor breakdown service, short-distance towing and other acts of mercy for its millions of members. Call ☎ 800-222-4357 for road service. AAA members can also pick up free road maps at AAA offices (1440 New York Ave NW, Suite 200; 5, D7; ☎ 942-2050) and might also qualify for discounts from a range of hotels and car rental companies.

PRACTICAL INFORMATION

Climate & When to Go

Washington is south of the Mason-Dixon Line, which divided northern free states from southern slave states before the Civil War, and its weather is proof that it's a southern town. Winters are mild, with occasional cold snaps and snowfalls that stop everything, and summers are hot and humid enough to slow down the town. In spring, blooming cherry trees draw huge crowds to the Mall and Tidal Basin. Fall is the best time to visit, when children are in school and Congress is in session. High season runs from late March, when the cherry trees start to bloom, to mid-July, when the heat becomes oppressive; book early if you plan on visiting during this period. Expect crowds at the most popular attractions any time of the year.

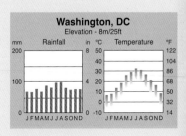

Tourist Information

Tourist Information Abroad

The US lacks overseas tourist information offices; try the Washington-based sources listed below.

Local Tourist Information

The Washington, DC, Convention and Tourism Corporation (WCTC; 1212 New York Ave NW, Suite 600; 5, D8; ☎ 789-7000; e www.washington.org) provides a wide range of tourist information, from maps and brochures about city sights to online hotel and restaurant reservations to guides that you can download free from the website. The office is open weekdays 9am-5pm.

The District of Columbia Chamber of Commerce maintains its own visitor information center in the Ronald Reagan Trade Center (1300 Pennsylvania Ave NW; 5, F7; ☎ 347-7201; e www.dcchamber.org); it's open Monday to Saturday 8am-6pm. Visitors can get maps, ask questions, take a virtual tour of the city on one of the computer terminals and buy Metro passes.

Embassies

Australia
    1601 Massachusetts Ave NW, Washington, DC 20008 (5, A5; ☎ 797-3000; after-hours emergency number for Australian nationals ☎ 888-239-3501)

Canada
    501 Pennsylvania Ave NW, Washington, DC 20001 (5, F10; ☎ 682-1740)

France
    4101 Reservoir Rd NW, Washington, DC 20007 (4, C3; ☎ 944-6000)

Germany
    4645 Reservoir Rd NW, Washington, DC 20007 (4, C2; ☎ 298-4393)

Ireland
    2234 Massachusetts Ave NW, Washington, DC 20008 (4, C6; ☎ 462-3939)

Mexico
    1911 Pennsylvania Ave NW, Washington, DC 20006 (5, C3; ☎ 728-1600)

New Zealand
    37 Observatory Circle, Washington, DC 20008 (4, B4; ☎ 328-4800)

South Africa
    3051 Massachusetts Ave NW, Washington DC 20008 (4, B4; ☎ 232-4400)

UK
    3100 Massachusetts Ave NW, Washington DC 20008 (4, B4; ☎ 588-7800)

Money

Currency
US dollars are the only currency accepted. The US dollar is divided into 100 cents (¢). Coins come in denominations of 1¢ (penny), 5¢ (nickel), 10¢ (dime), 25¢ (quarter), 50¢ (half-dollar) and $1. Although a new dollar coin has just been issued, one rarely sees dollar coins or half-dollar coins. Quarters are the handiest coins, for vending machines, parking meters and the like.

US bills are all the same color and the same size. They come in $1, $2, $5, $10, $20, $50 and $100 denominations, but $2 bills are extremely rare. Some shops won't accept notes in denominations higher than $20.

Credit Cards
Major credit cards are accepted just about everywhere. You'll need them for certain transactions, such as renting a car, registering for a hotel room or buying tickets to a play or sporting event. Visa and MasterCard are the most commonly accepted, followed by American Express and Discover cards. Carry copies of your credit card numbers separately from your cards. Should your cards be lost or stolen, be sure to contact the company immediately:

American Express	☎ 800-528-4800
Diners Club	☎ 800-234-6377
Discover	☎ 800-347-2683
MasterCard	☎ 800-826-2181
Visa	☎ 800-336-8472

ATMs
ATMs are good alternatives to traveler's checks. You can find them all over town – in airports and train stations, outside banks and inside grocery stores. Almost all accept cards from the Cirrus, Star and Global Access networks. Charges to use ATMs that belong to other

banks than your own start at 50¢; most machines will disclose the amount of the charge and ask whether you want to proceed before they give you your cash.

Changing Money

Banks usually offer better rates than exchange offices. Major banks change money during normal business hours. American Express has several DC locations, including one in Dupont Circle (1150 Connecticut Ave NW; 5, B4; ☎ 457-1300; Mon-Fri 9am-6pm) and one in Mazza Gallerie over in Friendship Heights (5300 Wisconsin Ave NW; 6, D4; ☎ 362-4000). Thomas Cook has an office downtown (1800 K Street NW; 5, C4; ☎ 800-287-7362) and counters at National and Dulles airports. Overseas visitors can also use their ATM cards to get US cash almost anywhere, at bank exchange rates.

Tipping

Tipping is customary in bars, restaurants, and better hotels. Tip your server at a restaurant 15% (unless the service is terrible) and 20% or more if the service is great. Tip the bartender $1 for one or two drinks, or 15% if you're buying a round. Tip taxi drivers $1 on a fare of $6 or less, 10% from there on up. Baggage carriers should get $1 per bag, and valet parkers $2 when they hand you the keys to your car. Doormen should get $1-2 to get you a cab, the concierge at your hotel $5 or more for booking a table or theater tickets, and the maid at your hotel $1-2 per night.

Discounts

Most attractions in Washington are free, so there's little need to look for discount tickets. Stretch your dollars with free concerts on the Mall during the summer and on major national holidays.

Student & Youth Cards

Most student and teacher discounts are reserved for students and teachers from local institutions.

Senior Cards

Seniors can get discounts at some sights and hotels. Ask if you don't see a sign. Some discounts apply to ages 50 and over, others to ages 60 or 65 and over. Seniors with a Medicare card or a Metro senior ID can buy special reduced-fare cards for Metrorail at the Metro headquarters (600 5th St NW; 5, E10) or at the Metro Center (12th & G Sts NW; 5, D8).

Travel Insurance

A policy covering theft, loss, medical expenses and compensation for cancellation or delays in your travel arrangements is highly recommended. If items are lost or stolen, make sure you get a police report right away – otherwise your insurer might not pay up.

Opening Hours

Most offices are open weekdays from 8:30 or 9am to 5 or 5:30pm. Most shops are open Monday to Saturday 10am-7pm, Sunday noon-6pm. Restaurants are usually open daily, serving lunch 11:30am-2pm and dinner 5:30-10pm (sometimes later, especially on weekends). Most shops are open on public holidays (except for Thanksgiving, Christmas and New Year's Day), but banks, schools and government offices are usually closed.

Public Holidays

Jan 1	New Year's Day
3rd Mon in Jan	Martin Luther King Jr Day
Jan 20 every 4th year	Inauguration Day

3rd Mon in Feb	Presidents' Day
Mar/Apr	Easter Sunday
Last Mon in May	Memorial Day
Jul 4	Independence Day
1st Mon in Sep	Labor Day
2nd Mon in Oct	Columbus Day
Nov 11	Veterans' Day
4th Thurs in Nov	Thanksgiving Day
Dec 25	Christmas Day

Time

Washington lies in the US Eastern time zone, 5hrs behind GMT/UTC. Eastern Daylight Saving Time (EDT) runs from the first Sunday of April, when clocks are advanced 1hr, to the last Saturday of October, when they're turned back 1hr. During the rest of the year, Eastern Standard Time (EST) is used. When it's noon in Washington, it's

noon in New York

9am in Los Angeles

5pm in London

7pm in Johannesburg (EDT) or 6pm (EST)

6am (following day) in Auckland (EDT) or 4am (EST)

4am (following day) in Sydney (EDT) or 2am (EST)

Electricity

Electricity in the US is 110V and 60Hz. Plugs have either two or three pins (always two flat, with an optional round grounding pin). Adaptors for European and South American plugs are common. Australians should bring their own adaptors.

Weights & Measures

Ever antagonized by the metric systems, Americans are sticking with the so-called English system. Distances come in inches, feet, yards and miles; dry weights are gauged in ounces, pounds and tons; liquid volumes are described in pints, quarts and gallons. The US gallon contains about 20% less liquid than the imperial gallon because it amounts to only 4 quarts. See the conversion table on p. 122.

Post

Postal Rates

You can purchase stamps at post offices or even at certain ATMs. At press time, domestic first-class mail cost 34¢ for letters up to 1oz (and 22¢ for each additional ounce). The standard rate for postcards is 20¢. International airmail to destinations other than North America (Canada and Mexico) costs 60¢ per letter, 55¢ per postcard. Postage on half-ounce letters to Canada is 48¢; to Mexico, it's 40¢.

Opening Hours

The National Capitol Post Office, in the National Postal Museum building (1st St NE; 5, D13; ☎ 523-2628), is open weekdays 7am-midnight and weekends 7am-8pm. The station in the Old Post Office Pavilion (Pennsylvania Ave & 12th St NW; 5, F8; ☎ 653-5300) is open weekdays 7:30am-5:30pm, Saturday 8am-12:30pm. Other branches are listed in the Government Listings section of the white pages in the telephone directory.

Telephone

Almost all public telephones in the Greater Washington area are coin-operated, although there are some pay phones that accept phone cards, and even some that accept credit cards. Phone booths are still relatively common, despite the recent explosion in mobile phone service. Local calls generally cost 35¢. Calls to outlying suburbs will cost more.

Phone Cards

Newsstands and pharmacies sell prepaid phone cards, but be careful to buy one issued by a reputable long-distance carrier. Lonely Planet's eKno Communication Card, specifically aimed at travelers, provides competitive international calls (avoid using it for local calls), messaging services and free email. Log on to [e] www.ekno.lonelyplanet.com for information on joining and accessing the service.

Mobile Phones

The US uses a variety of mobile phone systems, only one of which is remotely compatible with systems used outside North America. Most North American travelers can use their mobiles in Washington, but they should check with their carriers about roaming charges.

Country & City Area Codes

The US country code is ☎ 1. The area code for the District of Columbia is ☎ 202. (Unless otherwise noted, all phone numbers in this book fall within the 202 area code.) The Maryland suburbs lie in area code ☎ 301, and the Virginia suburbs sport two area codes: ☎ 703 and ☎ 571. If you're dialing a number outside the area you're calling from, be sure to dial a 1 first.

Useful Numbers

Directory Assistance	☎ 411
International Directory Assistance	☎ 412-555-1515
International Dialing Code	☎ 011
Operator	☎ 0
International Operator	☎ 00
Collect (Reverse-Charge)	☎ 0
Operator-Assisted Calls	☎ 01 (+ the number; an operator then comes on)
Time	☎ 844-2525
Weather	☎ 301-936-1212

International Codes

For direct-dial, use ☎ 011 followed by:

Australia	☎ 61
Canada	☎ 1
France	☎ 33
Germany	☎ 49
Japan	☎ 81
New Zealand	☎ 64
South Africa	☎ 27
UK	☎ 44

Digital Resources

You can check your email at the public libraries, including the Martin Luther King Jr Memorial Library downtown (5, D8), at one of the local Internet cafés or at some copy services centers, such as Kinko's.

Internet Service Providers

America Online is the 800lb gorilla of ISPs in the US. Two other major ISPs in the country are Microsoft Network and Earthlink/Mindspring. Access AOL at ☎ 464-0260 or 715-2100, MSN at ☎ 222-1121 or Earthlink at ☎ 360-4492.

Internet Cafes

If you can't access the Internet from the place where you're staying, head up to cyberSTOP Café (1513 17th St NW; 4, C7; ☎ 234-2470; 7am-midnight), where docking costs $1.99-3.99 and computer rental runs $5.99 per half-hour (or $7.99/hr). Cyberlaptops.com (1636 R St NW, 2nd Floor; 4, C6; ☎ 462-7195) is a computer repair and laptop-rental service with several workstations available ($2 per half-hour). At Kramerbooks (1517 Connecticut Ave NW; 4, C7; ☎ 387-1400), there's only one terminal, but it's free.

Useful Sites

The website for Lonely Planet ([e] www.lonelyplanet.com) offers a speedy link to DC websites. Other online resources you could try include the following:

Washington Post
e www.washingtonpost.com

Washington, DC, Convention and Tourism Corporation
e www.washington.org

District of Columbia Chamber of Commerce
e www.dcchamber.org

Georgetown Business Improvement District
e www.georgetowndc.com

CitySync

CitySync *Washington, DC,* Lonely Planet's digital guide for Palm OS handheld devices, allows quick searching, sorting and bookmarking of hundreds of Washington's attractions, clubs, hotels, restaurants and more – all pinpointed on scrollable street maps. Purchase or demo CitySync *Washington, DC* at e www.citysync.com.

Doing Business

All of the Kinko's stores downtown (325 7th St NW; 5, F9; ☎ 347-8730; also at 1612 K St NW; 5, C5; ☎ 466-3777) offer basics such as workstations, fax machines, copiers and Internet access 24hrs daily. Other Kinko's locations have the same facilities but close at different times in the evening. Most large hotels and some smaller ones contain business centers where you can find workstations, fax machines, copiers and Internet access.

Travelers looking for information about doing business in the area should contact the District of Columbia Chamber of Commerce (1213 K St NW; 5, C8; ☎ 347-7201; e www.dcchamber.org).

Newspapers & Magazines

Washington has two daily newspapers: the *Washington Post*, of Pentagon Papers and Watergate fame, and the *Washington Times*. Under the leadership of the late Katharine Graham and her son Donald, the *Post* has become one of the best newspapers in the US, providing thorough coverage of everything from Capitol Hill intrigues to suburban sewer-board hearings. Check Friday's Weekend section for event listings. The *Times* is owned by the Unification Church, which accounts for its heavy conservative tone. In size and quality, it runs a distant second to the *Post*.

The Washingtonian, a glossy monthly, caters to the professional classes, with restaurant reviews, cultural news and real estate ads. The *Washington City Paper* is a free weekly with strong entertainment coverage; it's available in news boxes around town. The free weeklies *Washington Blade* and *MW* serve the gay and lesbian community.

Radio

Washington boasts two National Public Radio stations: WETA (90.9FM), which also plays classical music, and WAMU (88.5FM). For conventional news radio, try WTOP (107.7FM). Go to WWDC (101.1FM) for classic rock and WHSF (99.1FM) for more alternative rock. Hip-hop and soul inhabit WKYS (93.9FM) and WPGC (95.5FM). The 'Quiet Storm' (easy listening with a touch of soul) blows on WHUR (96.3FM), and classical lives on at WGMS (103.5FM)

TV

Every national network or quasi-network has a local affiliate in DC, so you won't have trouble finding familiar programming as you scan the channels. There are also three PBS (public television) affiliates: WMPT (Channel 22), WETA (Channel 26) and WHUT (Channel 32). WHUT also carries some Spanish-language programming.

Photography & Video

For equipment and film, head to Ritz Camera downtown (1750 L St NW; 5, C4; ☎ 861-7710) or Best Buy in Pentagon City (1201 S Hayes St, Suite B, Arlington; 4, J4; ☎ 703-414-7090), which offers a larger selection. For processing, try one of the branches of Moto-Photo (1819 H St NW; 5, D4; ☎ 822-9001; also located at 1601 Connecticut Ave NW; 4, C6; ☎ 797-9035), a reliable local chain. Overseas visitors shopping for videos should note that the US uses NTSC, which is incompatible with PAL (UK and Australasia) and SECAM formats (Western Europe).

Health

Immunizations
No immunizations are required to enter the US.

Precautions
You can drink the water in Washington (although many residents prefer the bottled stuff) and you can breathe the air. If you do exercise or spend a lot of time in Washington's infamous heat and humidity during the summer, drink plenty of fluids and take breaks.

The usual precautions apply when it comes to sex. Condoms are available at pharmacies and most corner stores. Use them.

Insurance & Medical Treatment
Overseas visitors should have medical insurance before they come to DC, as medical care can be very expensive in the US; many doctors and hospitals insist on payment before treatment.

Medical Services
In an emergency, dial ☎ 911 for an ambulance. Note that emergency room charges, like other medical costs, are extremely expensive.

The George Washington University Hospital (901 23rd St NW; 5, C2; ☎ 994-1000) is an excellent institution, convenient to both downtown and the Northwest quadrant. (It's where they took Ronald Reagan when John Hinckley shot him outside the Washington Hilton.) Other hospitals in the area include:

Children's National Medical Center
111 N Michigan Ave NW (4, A9; ☎ 884-5000)

Georgetown University Medical Center
3800 Reservoir Rd NW (4, C3; ☎ 687-2000)

Howard University Hospital
2041 Georgia Ave at Florida Ave NW (4, B9; ☎ 865-6100)

Pharmacies
CVS and Rite Aid are major pharmacy chains with outlets all over town. The CVS branches at 6 Dupont Circle NW (5, A3; ☎ 785-1466) and 4555 Wisconsin Ave NW (6, E5; ☎ 537-1587) are open 24hrs. You'll find a Rite Aid in the Executive Office Building (1034 15th St NW; 5, C6; ☎ 296-6171). For other store locations, call CVS at ☎ 800-746-7287 or Rite Aid at ☎ 800-748-3243.

Toilets

All the large federal museums and offices have large, clean, accessible restrooms. If you need a restroom when you're strolling the streets, head inside a large hotel, shopping mall or public building.

Safety Concerns

Washington may not be the murder capital of the country any longer, but it is a big city and neighborhoods can change from gracious to dangerous within a block. Don't carry huge amounts of cash, and lock up what you don't need if your hotel has a safe or safety deposit boxes. Don't carry your wallet in your backpack or back pocket. Stay out of empty streets after dark.

The main visitor areas around the Mall, Georgetown, Dupont Circle and Adams-Morgan are very safe during the day and quite safe at night if you stick to the main streets (use 18th St to walk between Adams-Morgan and Dupont Circle, M St or Pennsylvania Ave to walk to Georgetown).

Capitol Hill gets dicey east of 7th St, as do much of the Southeast and Southwest quadrants below I-395. Take care visiting these areas during the day, and take taxis after dark, even if there's a Metro station nearby. The same applies to the borderlands between Northwest and Northeast DC – again, stick to the brightly lit cross streets like P St or U St. Stay east of 13th St NW if you're visiting the Shaw area after dark, unless you're traveling with locals.

Lost Property
If you lose something on the Metro, call ☎ 962-1165.

Keeping Copies
Make photocopies of all important documents and keep some with you separate from the originals, but always leave a copy at home. You can store details of documents in Lonely Planet's free online Travel Vault, password-protected and accessible around the world at ⓔ www.ekno.lonelyplanet.com.

Emergency Numbers

Police, Fire, Ambulance ☎ 911
Police Information ☎ 727-1010
Rape Crisis Line ☎ 333-7273

Women Travelers

Women are as safe in Washington as in most big American cities. The usual precautions apply: pay attention to surroundings and take extra care walking at night. On the street, especially after dark, men might make harassing comments, but that's generally about the limit if you just ignore them and keep moving.

Tampons and pads are widely available. The contraceptive pill is available by prescription only; the 'morning after' pill is technically available by prescription, but it's harder to come by.

Gay & Lesbian Travelers

Washington has a large gay and lesbian community, mainly centered on Dupont Circle (particularly along P St west of the Circle and 17th St between P and R Sts). Based on the 2000 census, DC, Arlington and Alexandria were three of the 10 US jurisdictions with the greatest number of same-sex households. It's estimated that the DC area ranks fourth in the country in number of heavily gay neighborhoods, after San Francisco, Los Angeles and New York.

For information on gay and lesbian nightlife, see Gay & Lesbian Washington (p. 96).

Information & Organizations
Washington has two gay weeklies: the *Washington Blade*, which focuses on community politics, and *MW*, which focuses on community recreation. Both are available free on newsstands and at bookstores around town. The Washington, DC,

Convention and Tourism Corporation publishes its own gay and lesbian guide to the city, available for free on its website (**e** www.washington.org). The Gay & Lesbian Hotline (☎ 833-3234) provides phone counseling and referrals.

For HIV-related questions, call the AIDS Hotline (☎ 800-342-2437). For other health questions, try the Whitman-Walker Clinic (1407 S St NW; 4 C7; ☎ 797-3500), which serves the gay and lesbian community with general health care, as well as HIV/AIDS matters.

Senior Travelers

A good public transit network, easily navigable terrain and wide range of attractions render Washington a good destination for seniors.

Information & Organizations
The DC Office on Aging (441 4th St NW; 5, E11; ☎ 724-5626) has a free directory of businesses that give senior discounts; it's open weekdays 8:15am-4:45pm. The American Association of Retired Persons (AARP; 601 E St NW; 5, E10; ☎ 800-424-3410; **e** www.aarp.org), a lobbying group for Americans ages 50 and older, offers hotel and car rental discounts.

Disabled Travelers

Washington is also a good destination for the mobility-impaired. All Metro trains and 70% of Metrobuses are wheelchair-accessible. Disabled people unable to use public transit can use MetroAccess, a door-to-door service, by calling ☎ 301-562-5361 to applying for a pass.

Most of the major sights and most major hotels and restaurants also offer wheelchair access. The picturesque brick sidewalks of Georgetown and Capitol Hill might present obstacles, but most of the rest of the sidewalks of the city are in good repair, with curb cuts at the corners.

Information & Organizations
The Washington, DC, Convention and Tourism Corporation (☎ 789-7000; **e** www.washington.org) distributes a fact sheet on accessibility at attractions, hotels and restaurants. Gallaudet University (4, D11), the national liberal arts college for the deaf and hard of hearing, hosts lectures and cultural events for the deaf (☎ TTY 651-5000; **e** www.gallaudet.edu). Mobility International USA (PO Box 10767, Eugene, OR 97440; ☎ 541-343-1284; fax 541-343-6812) advises disabled travelers on mobility issues and runs education programs. The Society for the Advancement of Travelers with Handicaps (347 Fifth Ave, Suite 610, New York 10016; ☎ 212-447-7284; **e** www.sath.org) publishes the magazine *Open World* for disabled travelers.

Language

Although they speak American English in DC, acronyms and insider terms can sometimes bewilder visitors. It's a quick leap from USA to DOD (Department of Defense) to POTUS (President of the United States). A couple of expressions you're likely to see in print or hear on the street include:

The Beltway – literally, I-495/95, the highway that runs around the District and inner suburbs. 'Inside the Beltway' denotes locals' point of view, 'outside the Beltway' refers to the rest of the USA.

cave dweller – pre-WWII Washington society; generally refers to residents of the streets on either side of Rock Creek Park

The District, DC – the city of Washington, as opposed to the suburbs

Conversion Table

Clothing Sizes
Measurements approximate only; try before you buy.

Women's Clothing

Aust/NZ	8	10	12	14	16	18
Europe	36	38	40	42	44	46
Japan	5	7	9	11	13	15
UK	8	10	12	14	16	18
USA	6	8	10	12	14	16

Women's Shoes

Aust/NZ	5	6	7	8	9	10
Europe	35	36	37	38	39	40
France only	35	36	38	39	40	42
Japan	22	23	24	25	26	27
UK	3fi	4fi	5fi	6fi	7fi	8fi
USA	5	6	7	8	9	10

Men's Clothing

Aust/NZ	92	96	100	104	108	112
Europe	46	48	50	52	54	56
Japan	S		M	M		L
UK	35	36	37	38	39	40
USA	35	36	37	38	39	40

Men's Shirts (Collar Sizes)

Aust/NZ	38	39	40	41	42	43
Europe	38	39	40	41	42	43
Japan	38	39	40	41	42	43
UK	15	15fi	16	16fi	17	17fi
USA	15	15fi	16	16fi	17	17fi

Men's Shoes

Aust/NZ	7	8	9	10	11	12
Europe	41	42	43	44fi	46	47
Japan	26	27	27.5	28	29	30
UK	7	8	9	10	11	12
USA	7fi	8fi	9fi	10fi	11fi	12fi

Weights & Measures

Weight
1kg = 2.2lb
1lb = 0.45kg
1g = 0.04oz
1oz = 28g

Volume
1 liter = 0.26 US gallons
1 US gallon = 3.8 liters
1 liter = 0.22 imperial gallons
1 imperial gallon = 4.55 liters

Length & Distance
1 inch = 2.54cm
1cm = 0.39 inches
1m = 3.3ft = 1.1yds
1ft = 0.3m
1km = 0.62 miles
1 mile = 1.6km

lonely planet

Lonely Planet is the world's most successful independent travel information company, with offices in Australia, the US, UK and France. Based on its reputation for comprehensive, reliable travel information, Lonely Planet is a print and electronic publishing leader, featuring over 650 titles and 22 series catering for travelers' individual needs.

At Lonely Planet we believe that travelers can make a positive contribution to the countries they visit – if they respect their host communities and spend their money wisely. Since 1986 a percentage of the income from books has been donated to aid and human rights projects.

www.lonelyplanet.com

For news, views and free subscriptions to print and email newsletters, and a full list of LP titles, click on Lonely Planet's award-winning website.

On the Town

A romantic escape to Paris or a mad shopping dash through New York City, the locals' secret bars or a city's top attractions – whether you have 24 hours to kill or months to explore, Lonely Planet's On the Town products will give you the lowdown.

Condensed guides are ideal pocket guides for when time is tight. Their quick-view maps, full-color layout and opinionated reviews help short-term visitors target the top sights and discover the very best eating, shopping and entertainment options a city has to offer.

For more in-depth coverage, **City guides** offer insights into a city's character and cultural background as well as providing broad coverage of where to eat, stay and play. **CitySync**, a digital guide for your handheld unit, allows you to reference stacks of opinionated, well-researched travel information. Portable and durable **City Maps** are perfect for locating those backstreet bars or hard-to-find local haunts.

'Ideal for a generation of fast movers.'

– *Gourmet Traveller* on Condensed guides

Condensed Guides

- Amsterdam
- Athens
- Barcelona
- Bangkok (Sept 2002)
- Boston
- California
- Chicago
- Dublin
- Frankfurt
- Hong Kong
- London
- Los Angeles (Oct 2002)
- New York City
- Paris
- Prague
- Rome
- San Francisco (Oct 2002)
- Singapore (Oct 2002)
- Sydney
- Tokyo
- Venice (June 2002)
- Washington, DC

index

See also separate indexes for Places to Eat (p. 126), Places to Stay (p. 127), Shops (p. 127) and Sights with map references (p. 128).

PLACES TO EAT

PLACES TO STAY

SHOPS

sights – quick index